GUARDHOUSE, GALLOWS and GRAVES

The Trial and Execution of Indian Prisoners
of the Modoc Indian War by the U. S. Army
1873

Compiled by Francis S. Landrum

With foreword by Pat McMillan

Cover photo:
Schonchin and Captain Jack in chains.

Published by
Klamath County Museum
1415 Main Street
Klamath Falls, Oregon 97601
1988

Library of Congress
Catalog Card Number: 88-81845

ISBN   0-9619719-0-8

TABLE of CONTENTS

ILLUSTRATIONS

MAPS and CHARTS

FOREWORD

This book was conceived quite innocently during a conversation with the author when each of us was giving our opinion of what the future plans for the Fort Klamath Museum and Park should entail. Having only the bare rudiments of the land site to build on, the historic interpretation requires considerable imagination and a great deal of reliance on written documentation and historic photographs. Francis S. (Van) Landrum has a wealth of both. It was he who surveyed the pasture and relocated the flagpole described as "the landmark which was visible for miles." From the flagpole, Van set up his transit and mapped the locations of the buildings which made up Fort Klamath. The picture that comes to mind is of a crude log enclosure, cramped quarters, and ponderous gates which are closed in "the nick of time." Erase that scene.

The site of Fort Klamath is located in a valley of luxuriant green grass which seems to stretch for miles. The hills surrounding it are filled with statuesque pines. Each of these characteristics was utilized in the establishment of the fort — native grasses to feed the cavalry horses and lumber for construction. A simple, white board fence surrounded the core area of a fort which sprawled over many acres. Whitewashed, sawn-board buildings bordered the parade grounds. Perhaps if you close your eyes you can hear the stamp of the horses, the birdsong in the meadow, and the twitter of laughter from the ladies at the gazebo.

Why, then, mar this peaceful scene with the ugly realities of the Modoc Indian War? This question is asked throughout history, when a chain of events suddenly erupts in warfare.

This book was compiled from arduous research which included obscure, unpublished sources. Van agreed "to fill in the historical gap" with this publication only if the proceeds generated would be set aside to be used in perpetuity for the continued operation of the Klamath County Museums. (A nonprofit supporting fund has been established for this purpose.) The author seeks no fame or profit and has given unstintingly of his time, talent, and expertise to record an historic event that played an all-important role in shaping the history of the Klamath country.

Neither Van nor I had ever ventured into the field of writing and realized this undertaking needed a critical, unbiased eye. We are indebted and grateful for the editing expertise of Helen Freiser, who used her professional background to such great benefit in editing the manuscript.

Finally, my debt to the author for producing this book can never be repaid. The fact that he is still a friend is miraculous. To Patty, his wife: thank you for graciously enduring the frustrations and privations of an author's wife.

With these mere words, I express my gratitude, "Thank You."

Now, let's get on with the story.

Pat McMillan, Director
Klamath County Museums

INTRODUCTION

Several years ago, a scrapbook collection of newspaper clippings surfaced which shed new light on the final days of the Army-Modoc struggle. A series of dispatches from the *Bellows Falls Times,* Bellows Falls, Vermont, accent the last hours of the chase to capture the fleeing Modocs, the circumstances of their trial by military commission, and the report of the ritual of the execution of the condemned victims. Included in the same scrapbook are isolated returns saved from the San Francisco *Evening Bulletin*, the San Francisco *Chronicle*, and the Eureka, California *Times*.

Lt. George W. Kingsbury, an erstwhile resident of Bellows Falls, was the *Bellows Falls Times* correspondent. Lt. Kingsbury was a member of the military commission that tried the accused Modoc Indians. He was the adjutant of the command that carried out the sentence of the tribunal in hanging four adjudged-guilty Modocs. That some of his dispatches read almost word for word as the returns of the correspondent for the *Chronicle*, suggests some type of working arrangement with William Bunker, the correspondent. Perhaps the newly devised "pool-reporting", which was first used in the Modoc Indian War, was put to good use by the New Englander.

This writer has chosen the *Bellows Falls Times* articles to flesh out the spare skeleton supplied by both the *Chronicle* and the San Francisco *Call* for the coverage of those last days. Kingsbury's reports agree much better with the military record of those miserable times and more closely conform with certain features that were initially evident on the ground. Readers should be warned that the various reports filed in the last days of the Modocs' stay at Fort Klamath do not agree in all respects.

Each of Kingsbury's dispatches is more complete than those of competitive journals for the same date. Yet no transcript, minutes, or specific reference to deliberations during the conduct of the trial by the military commission is included in his reports. Appendix B contains a reprint of the official transcript of the trial.

Following are several notes with respect to the apparent double sets of ranks:

Most of the U. S. Army officers in the Modoc Indian war were veterans of the Civil War. Brevet ranks were bestowed on an officer for gallant or heroic conduct. The officer was entitled to wear the uniform of the brevet rank, but his pay remained that of his regular army rank. We can find a cited officer appearing under two different ranks in this document. A short table of both ranks for any one of several officers is given:

Name	Brevet Rank	Regular Rank
Civil War (pre-Modoc War) brevets:		
Jefferson C. Davis	major general	colonel, 23rd Inf.
Gillem, Alvan C.	major general	colonel, 1st Cav.
Wheaton, Frank	major general	lt. col. 21st Inf.
Mason, Edwin C.	brigadier general	major 21st Inf.
Pollock, Robert	colonel	captain 21st Inf.
Hoge, George B.	brigadier general	captain 12th Inf.
Post-Modoc War brevets (for Modoc and Nez Perce campaigns)		
Elliott, Washington L.	major general	lt. col. 1st Cav.
Green, John	brigadier general	major 1st Cav.

This monograph does not intend to record the myriad of facets incident to the Modoc Indian war. It was never a question of whether or not the conclusion would be a hanging, but a hanging of whom and how many? Rather it is a continuum of those details funnelling in a deadly convergence to a foregone conclusion — a multiple execution. Probably its most important purpose is to explain why there are four visible graves lying in the luxuriant meadow at old Fort Klamath. The truth in a legend springing from its roots toward an eternity must start somewhere. Hopefully, it is here.

Francis S. Landrum
Klamath Falls, Oregon
May, 1988

CHAPTER 1

A PEOPLE THREATENED

Many well-documented sources relate that a significant number of white immigrants were cruelly tortured or killed at the hands of the Modoc Indian tribe. Far less is recorded which displays the evidence that American revenge against the Modocs was as bloody, grisly, and horrible as that of the Indians. The true story of the timing of these atrocities has dimmed with the passage of time. Which was guilty of the first assault, the Modoc or the white?

Traditionally, invading whites — Europeans and, later, Americans — considered any non-settled land in the transmontane west as fair game for taking. Although the American Indian recognized exclusive use of any territory which could be held by force, ownership of land, per se, was never enforced or questioned prior to the several Federal Indian treaties.

Framers of the United States Constitution specifically reserved all treaty-making powers to the federal executive with the senate retaining the responsibility to advise and consent. To this day, many Indian treaties, especially including the Klamath Lake Treaty of October 14, 1864, and the Council Butte Treaty of August 12, 1865, repose in the Foreign and Diplomatic Branch of the National Archives.

These conventions, when concluded, effectively extinguished Indian title. In theory, the agreement whereby the Indians retained only a portion of their range over which the tribe had roamed for uncounted millenia, seemed a fair and workable policy to the white faction. Indian consideration furnished in the exchange was the tribe's ceding a parcel of land as described in the words and handwriting of the Federal representative.

With magnificent largesse the treaty writer promised the tribal chiefs and headmen exclusive occupation of either a portion of its prior range or a part of the domain of another tribe. Through this device all lands yielded by the Indian signatories, approved by the U.S. Senate, and proclaimed by the Executive, became sovereign to the United States of America and remained in inventory until such time as the government chose to dispose of them.

Clearing and quietting title to massive blocks of "uncivilized wilderness" was the real reason for entering into treaties and conventions with Indian nations, tribes, and bands. Federal Indian policy envisioned an unchallenged acquisition of an unreasonably large domain without the necessity of any great outlay of consideration. Getting the tribe onto the reservation was a valued by-product to the Federal bureau. But clearing title to the Indian real property was not enough. The Indian people themselves must be moved onto a reservation—a corral, if you will— and be protected both from white usurpers and threats from other tribes. Both the Klamath Lake and Council Butte treaties were sealed on the part of the chiefs and headmen in a regular fashion. A secretary with a legible hand of penmanship wrote the document. Each chief's and headman's name was written clearly and phonetically spelled. As no chief or headman could read or write English or any other language, he simply marked "X, his mark" in the presence of attesting witnesses.

Example: "Poo Sak Sult his (X) mark (seal)". Mbushakshaltko was a Klamath Indian chief who lived on the Williamson River and whose name meant "Obsidian", or "Maker of obsidian tools." He was the "Krupp of the Klamaths".

Thus, Keint-poses, better known by his applied name of Captain Jack, and his adherents maintained that they never agreed to leave their homeland and move some forty or so miles to be bandied about on the turf of the Klamaths. Treaty papers (qv) clearly display Jack's rather passable "X", followed by a segment of a legal seal (bright red on the original) intended to impress the solemnity of his acquiescence to the import of the document.

All of which brings up a question: Can an "X, his mark" be forged? Probably Jack's was not, but more certainly, the Modocs of Jack's band never knowingly yielded their beloved Lost River circle river/swamp/lake system for a new and different home among their northern adversaries.

Modoc land was mostly dry, sagebrush and juniper prairie, and shallow Great Basin lakes well-fringed with cattails and tules, and was the home of the pronghorn antelope, sage hen, and mullet. Klamath Indian environs had more brown bear, pine marten, and salmon and trout in rather fast-running streams. Modoc hills were rock, sagebrush, and rimrock; Klamath hills were splendid slopes of ponderosa pine trees.

In arriving at that question and answer, one must keep in mind that the Klamaths and Modocs are the only peoples within fifty to ninety miles of either who spoke, and still do speak, the same language. Rogues, Snakes, Paiutes, Shastas, Pit Rivers — all use a language unintelligible to the Klamaths and Modocs.

For many years since 1818, pretensions of the United States, Great Britain, Spain, Mexico, Russia, and France have served as liens on the west coast of the North American continent. Label these European and American attachments as "exterior claims" as opposed to the "interior claims" of the Indian.

One must consider the homeland of the Modoc tribe. Interestingly, the 42nd parallel of north latitude passes through the tribe's homeland separating both the domains and influence of the tribal branches into approximately equal parts, the Hot Creeks living south (California) of the parallel and Captain Jack's band living to the north (Oregon). This Indian occupation comprised the only interior claim against the land.

Exterior claims were manifold. Provision for joint British-American occupation of lands lying westerly from the "Stony Mountains" was spelled out by the 1818 Treaty of London — a document which, in 1828, was renewed for ten-year intervals. One year later, Spain and the United States concluded the Adams-Onis "Florida" Treaty, which defined the 42nd parallel as the northern line of Spanish sovereignty and the southern boundary of United States influence.

Spain was dropped from the contest for acquiring the

American northwest but, to some degree, was entrenched in Alta California. American sovereignty over lands in California and Nevada did not become a reality until the Convention of Guadalupe Hidalgo was consummated in 1848 between the United States and Mexico. Mexico had become the successor to Spain for lands lying south of the 42nd parallel.

Russian claims to portions of the Pacific West, specifically Fort Ross and Bodega Bay, were laid to rest through the convention of St. Petersburg in 1824. This is the document in which "fifty-four degrees and forty minutes of north latitude" was first written (in French). This parallel formed the southern boundary of Russian America and became the most southerly segment of the border between Alaska and Canada. That treaty was between Russia and the United States only; it did not include Great Britain.

French claims in North America were almost completely expunged in favor of Great Britain at the end of the French and Indian War, circa 1763. Yet, in the 1840's a French attache, du Mofras, spent some time on the west coast of North America hoping to find a flaw in the instruments which implied or defined Mexican, American, and British pretensions.

With the Treaty of Washington in June 1846, Great Britain finally yielded its interest in all western North American lands, south of the 49th parallel of north latitude, to the United States.

This discourse provides a different outlook as to the status of "owner(s)" of lands generally in Oregon and California both before and after California had gained statehood in 1850 and Oregon became a federal territory in 1848. On whose lands were the Modoc Indians living?

Before 1848, northern California and Nevada were Spanish and, in succession, Mexican lands. Thus any of the pre-1848 overland parties were trespassing on Mexico. This would include Ogden's "Snake Country" adventures, Fremont's second and third expeditions, and the various thrusts of Lieutenant Emmons, Bidwell-Bartleson, Jedediah Smith, etc. It's almost as if James W. Marshall's gold discovery at Coloma was held off until Guadalupe Hidalgo was in the bag.

If interior claims were honored and aboriginal title held, then any non-Mexican parties entering south of and near the 42nd parallel were poaching on Hot Creek Modoc lands. Similarly, any travel over lands north of and adjoining the 42nd parallel prior to 1846 was across Lost River Modoc territory.

Considering only exterior claims, entrance north of the parallel prior to 1846 was across jointly held British-American property, and in this domain lay the home of the Lost River Modoc Indians. Mark well— jointly held — not owned, not sovereign, not exclusive.

Any American complaint about depredations at the hands of the Indians pertained to an untrue pretension of ownership. No facts supported any type of implied easement, prescription, or the faintest color of title. An epidemic of trespass was met with what the Indians considered a just defense.

American occupation and settlement of western North America has been called a heroic effort of mammoth proportions in seeking out new homelands. The efforts of the immigrants required hard work, vigilance, and a constancy of devotion. Their thrusts have been lauded as the sterling faith of our forefathers.

If our forefathers were either American Indian or Mexican, must we not then truthfully declare that these same efforts at colonization were in reality a series of brutal, hobnailed thefts of their properties? Were not the cessions of vast estates through the treaty process merely an act of taking that which was desirable, by any means, fair or foul, which would tend to dispossess all but the white race?

Perhaps it will always be thus, but as a consequence, a Modoc tribe which was willing to fight for its home was wiped out. Usually the penalty for failure was death or exile. With Captain Jack's Modoc people it was both.

Captain Jack was cast by fate onto the horns of a dilemma. He had two difficult options: Should he keep faith and allegiance with the societal mores of his Modoc people, and fight numerically superior odds to defend them and their customs? Or should he, perhaps hypocritically, yield his and his peoples' homeland, independence, and freedom of choice to the ever-encroaching white trespassers?

The head chief of the Modoc Tribe, Old Schonchin, chose the latter; Jack and his band of renegades rallied for freedom, and suffered as losers in the senseless tragedy that followed.

Typically, the cruel consequences of a faulted federal policy were borne by those least able to afford them: an entire band of an aboriginal society and the military arm of a federal authority. Casualties suffered by white citizen and military were greater in number than there were Indians. The land then became "free", but only to those who, by self-evident truth, had been created equal. Nineteenth century philosophy could not abide by any belief that Indians were created equal.

Acting on a plea from Oregon Indian Superintendent Thomas B. Odeneal, Captain James Jackson's B Troop of 1st Cavalry struck the Modoc camp at pre-dawn, November 29, 1872. He and his men shot up and burned the Modoc camp because the Indians refused to return to that reservation established by a treaty to which they claimed they had never agreed. Indian thinking (at least on the part of the more volatile members of the band) called for revenge. Revenge was quick; in a foray around the north shore of Tule Lake, Modocs ended the lives of some fourteen settlers, all male, without any advance warning.

But that gang of Indians who left the bloody path all the way from Adams Point to Land's Island were not a part of the Modoc camp which Jackson had attacked. Who were they?

Conveniently overlooked by the white citizenry and military was an unwarned and unwarranted citizen attack on Hooker Jim's camp on the opposite (north, left bank) side of the river from Captain Jack's camp. Timing of the thrust followed Jackson's closely. Leaders of the citizens included James Thurber, Wendolen (or William) Nus, Joseph Penning, Dennis Crawley, O.A. Brown, and the ubiquitous Oliver C. Applegate.

No warning was given for the attack other than the noises of the Jackson skirmish upstream and across the river. No military man was involved in the north bank assault of

Photo no. 10. Brig. Gen. Edward R. S. Canby, commanding general of the Dept. of Columbia; murdered under a flag of truce by Modoc Indians at the Lava Beds. Landrum Collection.

Photo no. 15. The Reverend Doctor Eleazer Thomas, member of the Peace Commission; murdered under a flag of truce by Modoc Indians at the Lava Beds. Landrum Collection.

Photo no. 20. Alfred B. Meacham. Former Supt. of Indian Affairs for Oregon. Chairman of the Peace Commission. Attacked under a flag of truce and left for dead by Modoc Indians at the Lava Beds. Courtesy Elizabeth R. Stewart. Landrum Collection.

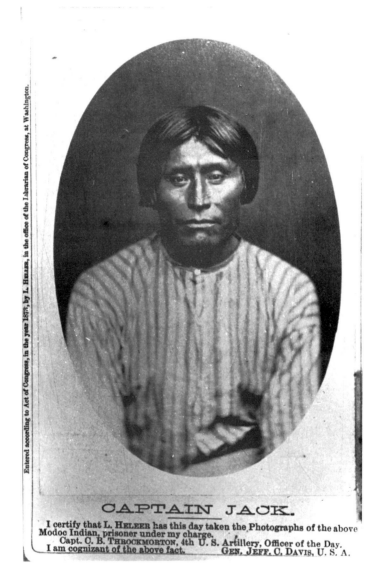

CAPTAIN JACK.

I certify that L. HELLER has this day taken the Photographs of the above
Modoc Indian, prisoner under my charge.
      Capt. O. B. THROCKMORTON, 4th U. S. Artillery, Officer of the Day.
I am cognizant of the above fact.   GEN. JEFF. C. DAVIS, U. S. A.

**Photo no. 25. Captain Jack, Modoc Indian. Hanged Oct. 3, 1873. Half
brother to Black Jim. Landrum Collection.**

SCHONCHIN.

I certify that L. HELLER has this day taken the Photographs of the above
Modoc Indian, prisoner under my charge.
    Capt. C. B. THROCKMORTON, 4th U. S. Artillery, Officer of the Day.
I am cognizant of the above fact,   GEN. JEFF. C. DAVIS, U. S. A.

**Photo no. 30. Schonchin John (aka, Schonchis), Modoc Indian. Hanged
Oct. 3, 1873. Landrum Collection.**

BOSTON CHARLEY.

I certify that L. HELLER has this day taken the Photographs of the above
Modoc Indian, prisoner under my charge.
    Capt. C. B. THROCKMORTON, 4th U. S. Artillery, Officer of the Day.
I am cognizant of the above fact.   GEN. JEFF. C. DAVIS, U. S. A.

**Photo no. 35. Boston Charley, Modoc Indian. Hanged Oct. 3, 1873.
Landrum Collection.**

BLACK JIM.

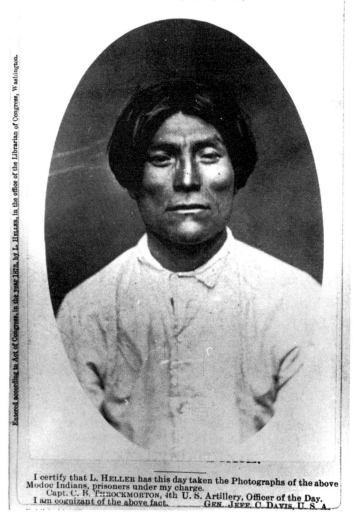

I certify that L. HELLER has this day taken the Photographs of the above Modoc Indians, prisoners under my charge.
Capt. C. B. THROCKMORTON, 4th U. S. Artillery, Officer of the Day.
I am cognizant of the above fact.   GEN. JEFF. C. DAVIS, U. S. A.

Photo no. 40. Black Jim, Modoc Indian. hanged Oct. 3, 1873. Half brother to Captain Jack. Lava Beds National Monument Collection.

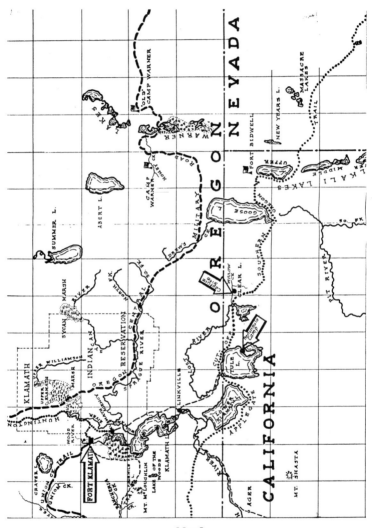

Map I

Hooker Jim's tribelet, nor had the citizenry been requested to aid Jackson's troop. Worse yet, after they had completely ravaged Hooker's camp, the citizens withdrew, failing to send out a 19th century Paul Revere. They lost two people, Nus and Thurber, yet no account has disclosed an Indian death.

In the ensuing excitement and in a display of utter negligence, none of the citizens stopped to think of the consequences of the Indians' rampaging easterly along the north shore of Tule Lake. Nor did any citizen equate the "wounded grizzly-bears" — Hooker's radicals — with sure and bloody vengeance. Quite a few entrymen (polite terminology for squatters) lived along the littoral plain; in this case, unaware what brutal butchery was to be their fate — and soon.

Hooker Jim was a "real mean" Indian, bloodthirsty and cruel. Later, in the ensuing Modoc Indian War, Hooker would be seen brutally killing the Yreka teenaged teamster, Eugene Hovey. He then, with fiendish delight, pounded the slain youth's head with lava rocks until it was "as thick as a man's hand".

The most redhanded of the culprits included Hooker Jim, Curly-Headed Doctor (the tribal shaman and one of Hooker's fathers-in-law), William the Wild Gal's Man, Ellen's Man George, Dave, and others, names unknown. Many of Hooker's party were called "Hot Creeks", as their tribal home grounds were the meadows bordering Hot Creek, Butte Creek, Willow Creek, and Cottonwood Creek, all in northern California and immediately south of Lower Klamath Lake.

Captain Jack's branch of the band was usually known as the Lost River Modocs because their haunts were generally located on the Lost River meanderings, including its source, Clear Lake, and its debouchment in Tule Lake. The Lost River faction also included several "Gumbatkni" or Rock Indians, so styled because their home was on the south side of Tule Lake in the fringes of the Lava Beds. (Kumme = cave, rock; kumbat = rock people; ckni or ckne = people from, and speaking the same language; stir thoroughly and it becomes kumbatckni or gumbatkni.)

Except for the bloody killings of Adam Shillinglow and Henry Miller, as far as is known, all of the November 29 murders of whites occurred on the Oregon side of the line (territory which in 1872 was a part of Jackson County). Within days, a Jackson County grand jury had indicted Captain Jack, Schonchin John, Scarface Charley and "John Does", without knowing who was actually involved. But an Indian is an Indian, and the only good Indians were dead Indians — so went the "civilized" thinking of that era. No evidence has ever surfaced to implicate any of the three above-named Indians in the November 29th slayings.

Neither Captain Jack nor the members of the Lost River band should have been named in the indictments handed down by the grand jury. When scurrying from the wrath of Jackson's troop, the Lost River band desperately paddled down the river and south across Tule Lake in dugout canoes. Their destination was Captain Jack's Stronghold, a tortuous mass of lava, spilled from the highland fumaroles and chimneys. Captain Jack, Scarface Charley, and Schonchin John were names well-known to the white community but no whites, with the possible exception of Alfred B. Meacham, Elisha Steele, and Judge Alex Rosborough, really cared who was named in the indictment. After all, what was the value of an Indian life?

CHAPTER 2

MURDER AT THE PEACE TENT

After the January 17, 1873 humiliating and total defeat of five companies of the U.S. Army and three companies of Oregon and California volunteer militia by a ragtag band of Modoc Indians, open warfare ceased. Federal Indian policy called for a halt in hostilities and the establishment of a Peace Commission. Negotiations were carried on for almost three months by a quasi-autonomous Peace Commission.

Members of the Commission had been appointed by President Grant on the recommendation of Columbus Delano, Secretary of the Interior. In practice, the Commission's voice and soul were actually those of the commanding general of the Military Department of the Columbia, Brig. Gen. Edward R. S. Canby. Dispatches very clearly show that the Peace Commission's actions were at all times directed by and subject to the veto of General Canby, and that he took his orders from the army chain of command.

The philosophy of the Indians was straightforward and logical, but impractical. In a mid-19th century social environment they were unable to understand why a white man, Ben Wright and his party, the perpetrators of a massacre of forty Modocs under a flag of truce in 1856, were never punished by white man's law.

An angry call came from the Oregonian bystanders who trumpeted loudly for indictments and trials. On the other hand, the rowdy gang of Hooker Jim and Curly-Headed Doctor knew full well that any yielding by a band of renegades would place them in jeopardy in a white tribunal, which at best was loaded against anyone of the red race.

At the time of the pitched battles that took place from January 17, 1873 to the following June 1st, whenever the deliberations touched on an Indian surrender (and what other subject was there to talk about — except extermination?) the Indian radicals carried the day and prevented

Captain Jack from yielding. With a loose organization unused to discipline and even less to any theme of loyalty, Jack was well aware that it mattered little what he did or said as far as ceding or surrendering. Probably the only loyalists who would have followed his lead would have been some of his Lost River Modocs.

During the protracted negotiations between the Modoc band and the Peace Commission, Captain Jack's actions were carefully monitored by the Hot Creek desperadoes. Curly-Headed Doctor, Hooker Jim, Bogus Charley, Steam boat Frank, Shacknasty Jim, Ellen's Man George, and other Hot Creeks counselled a course which would have Captain Jack slay the white chief, General Canby, while the other, lesser Modocs would fall upon the lesser whites, killing all they could.

If the "chief of the soldier-mans" could be slain, the remainder of the soldiers would run away. Simple. Whatever Jack did would be wrong so after enduring too much taunting and tormenting, he agreed to fire the first bullet.

On Good Friday, April 11, 1873, Captain Jack and Ellen's Man George shot General Canby to death while engaged in a Peace Commission session. With two shots, Boston Charley killed Commission member the Reverend Doctor Eleazar Thomas, and with the help of Steamboat Frank, stripped the body. Schonchin John, with the aid of Shacknasty Jim, and Black Jim, shot at Commission member Alfred B. Meacham five times. After Meacham had fallen, Boston Charley attempted to scalp him but was deterred by Toby Riddle yelling, "The soldiers are coming!" Toby's warning came while Boston Charley was engaged in the grisly process of trying to sever Meacham's ear, a logical alternative to scalping as Meacham was quite bald.

Indian agent and Commission member Leroy S. Dyar and interpreter Tazewell Frank Riddle successfully ran for their lives. Black Jim and Hooker Jim chased Dyar, and Riddle outdistanced the pursuing Ellen's Man George, Shacknasty Jim, and Barncho. Riddle's wife Toby, herself a full-blooded Modoc and first cousin to Captain Jack, was also employed by the federals as an interpreter. She remained on the scene and, even though knocked to the ground by Slolux, was protected from further harm by the quick action of Scarface Charley.

On the east side of the Stronghold a similar ruse was being enacted. Miller's Charley and Curly Haired Jack approached the infantry's line and called for an audience with the "white-man chief", Major Edwin C. Mason. Instead of Mason, the officer-of-the-day, Lt. William L. Sherwood, accompanied by Lt. William Boyle, walked out to receive the message from the Modocs.

When the officers were close enough to shoot, the Modocs levelled their rifles and fired. Both officers ran for their lives. Boyle escaped unhurt but Sherwood was shot in the upper thigh. Military medicine could not adequately cope with major fractures and Sherwood died on April 14, 1873.

An army which at one time bore the ratio of about 745 soldiers to 45 or 50 Indian warriors suffered horrible losses before it was able to drive the tribe out of the Lava Beds. Once in open rangeland its five troops of cavalry and the mounted light battery of artillery could seek out, destroy, or capture the Modocs.

Ellen's Man George was killed in the Indian retreat from the battle at Sorass Lake on the morning of May 10, 1873. Though far from either an Austerlitz or Antietam, it was the first victory for the army in the small, but intensely lethal, Indian war.

The cunning and strategy of Captain Jack and his lieutenants kept the tribe from capture from the 11th of April to the 22nd of May when sixtynine Hot Creeks, including sixteen warriors — men and boys from age twelve up — surrendered from their hiding place on Mahogany Mountain. Years before, John Fairchild first settled at the big spring at the northeastern toe of Mahogany Mountain. This spring, the source of Cottonwood Creek, was a favorite haunt of the Hot Creek band to which they homed without any undue effort or planning. Headquarters had suspected as much and had assigned Major Mason's infantry battalion to camp at the springs and receive any surrender. This was the first confirmation the army had of their suspicion that the tribe had split — the Hot Creeks fleeing to the Cottonwood and Willow Creek country and, for all that was known at that time, Captain Jack and his Lost River Modocs had vanished into thin air.

As would be known several days later, Jack and his followers also sought refuge at Willow Creek — another Willow Creek — emptying its waters into Lost River near its source in the northeast bay of Clear Lake. A casual observer studying western high desert geography might correctly conclude that many eastern Oregon/California creeks at one time or another had been called Willow Creek, Rock Creek, or Dry Creek.

CHAPTER 3

TREASON AND CAPTURE

In order to save their own lives, four of the surrendered Hot Creek band requested an audience with Brevet Maj. Gen. Jefferson C. Davis, Col., 23d Infantry, commanding general of the Department of the Columbia, recently appointed to succeed the slain Canby. Almost unreal to the mind of anyone with any sense of fair play and even rocking Davis back on his heels, Shacknasty Jim, Bogus Charley, Hooker Jim, and Steamboat Frank offered to serve as a scouting force for Davis in running down Captain Jack and his remaining force.

Davis was aware that he was conversing with probably the four worst traitorous, mean, and blood-thirsty scoundrels in the whole Modoc band, each deserving, as he put it, the halter. But he also could see a glimmer of the success which would be his if he could quickly locate and smoke out Jack. He also was a very experienced military commander and was humanitarian enough to recognize the saving of life which could result from effecting a quick conclusion to the war. And surely one can realize that the lives he intended to save were those of his troops.

Davis did not hesitate to arm and mount his turncoat "Bloodhounds", and heeded their advice to look for Jack at Willow Creek, the Clear Lake Willow Creek, twelve miles east of Tule Lake. An intrepid Davis openly displayed his bravery to his entire command when he rode away from the JF ranch in the company of the four Hot Creeks and John Fairchild. The little party rode past Capt. John Mendenhall's assembled artillery battalion bivouacked at the recently abandoned "Camp South of Tule Lake (Gillem's Camp)".

They rode on through the Stronghold in the Lava Beds, past Supply Camp at Scorpion Point, near Boyle's Camp on the peninsula, then across the intervening tableland to a destination at the ranch of Jesse Applegate and his family at the Fiddlers' Green spring on the north shore of Clear Lake.

Very little time was needed to confirm the hunches of the "Bloodhounds". Sometime during the tribe's containment in the Stronghold, prior to abandoning it on the early morning of April 17, hard-pressed Modocs openly discussed the options available to the Indians should they choose to flee, or be forced from, the Stronghold. Clear Lake's Willow Creek was probably the most remote location of the choices available to Jack. Even today, the last few miles of the route are liberally strewn with ungodly rough, rutted tracks and an almost impassible profusion of rocks and boulders, some as big as one's head.

Captain Jack and his people could not have remained hidden in that forlorn wasteland forever, but they could remain there longer than at whatever place would have been second choice. Of course, with no outside contact, Jack had no way of knowing of the "Bloodhounds" sale of the deadly intelligence to Davis. Eventually it became obvious that a trade had been consummated without defining it as such. All four "Bloodhounds" were granted freedom from the prisoner stockade, were not tried, were not hanged, but were exiled with the remaining renegades to Indian Territory.

On the other hand, of the Modocs who were hunted down by the "Bloodhounds", at least twelve were put in irons, and imprisoned in three dark little cells. Six were tried without counsel, found guilty, and sentenced to be executed by hanging. Of the six, four were hanged and the sentences of the remaining two were commuted to life imprisonment at Alcatraz Island.

In a later return, one of the traitors recounted his meeting with the Modoc chief: Jack immediately wanted to know why Hooker Jim was riding one of John Fairchild's horses. He also wanted to know in what devilishment the traitor was involved. And the return terminated with Hooker Jim's remark, "Jack was mad at me but he didn't say what for".

(Second dispatch)

APPLEGATE MANSION, Clear Lake, California, June 1st, 2 P.M. — This morning the troops at the camp in Langell's Valley, were divided into several parties and sent on scouts after the fleeing Modocs. Just as the scouting parties left, the Modoc captives, with the exception of Bogus Charley, Hooka Jim, Steamboat Frank, and Shacknasty Jim were sent to this ranch in charge of Lieutenant (Sydney W.) Taylor, of the Fourth Artillery and a small detachment of men, whither your correspondent also came. This is General Davis' headquarters at the present time. The Modocs are anxious to learn what disposition will be made of Schonchin.

(Dispatch)

—THE LATEST—

Captain Jack Surrenders — He is Brought Into Camp
His Appearance and Bearing — Every Inch a Chief

APPLEGATE'S HOUSE, CLEAR LAKE, June 1st — 3:30 P.M. — A series of prolonged yells and cheers aroused this camp from a pleasant siesta half an hour after the departure of my last courier. Gen. Davis, Gen. Wheaton, and other officers, and all the men rushed from the house and tents to find the cause of the uproar, and at once the whole camp was in commotion.

Down the level plain north of the house there was a grand cavalcade of mounted horsemen. The steeds rushed forward at a furious rate and soon neared the groups of spectators scattered about the premises. "Captain Jack is captured," shouted a sturdy Sergeant. Again the valley echoed with cheers and yells. The mounted command was that of Captain Perry. He had returned from a scout of twenty-three hours.

Three miles above the mouth of Willow Creek, at half-past 10 o'clock this morning, the Warm Spring scouts struck a hot trail, and after a brief search, Modocs were discovered. Col. Perry surrounded the Indian retreat. His men were bound to fight. Suddenly a Modoc shot out from the rocks with a white flag. He met a Warm Spring and said Jack wanted to surrender. Three scouts were sent to meet Jack. He came out cautiously, glanced about him a moment, and then as if giving up all hope, boldly came forward unarmed and held out his hand to his visitors; then two of his warriors, five squaws and seven children darted forth and joined him in the surrender.

The command that made this famous scout was the first squadron of the First Cavalry, Colonel D.(David) Perry, composed of troop F, Lieutenant (William H.) Miller; troop H, Major Trumbull (Joel G. Trimble) and medical officer Assistant Surgeon Duvitt (Calvin DeWitt). The guards (sic) (guides) were C. (Charles) Putnam and H. (Henry) H. Applegate.

Jack is about 40. He is 5 feet 8 inches high, and compactly built. He has a large and well-formed head, and a face full of individuality. Although dressed in old clothes, he looks every inch a chief. He does not speak to any one.

The Modocs are grouped in the field near the house and surrounded by a guard. Spectators peer into Jack's face with eager interest, but he heeds them not. He is still as a statue.

CHAPTER 4

THOUGHTS of COL. DAVIS[1]

(Dispatch)

— General Davis on the Modoc Question —

BOYLE'S CAMP, June 11th. — As General Davis' vigorous but enlightened proposition in reference to the treatment of the Modoc murderers imprisoned in this camp has provoked quite a comment in official and military circles, and believing that a clear statement of his ideas and contemplated action in the premises is of general public interest, I have obtained permission to publish the gist of an interview held yesterday afternoon [June 10, 1873]:

QUESTION — General Davis, will you have the kindness to relate to me your proposed action in regard to the Modoc murderers and the reasons therefor?
ANSWER — Certainly, sir. When I arrived in the field I found the troops engaged in a war with a band of Indian outlaws — murderers if you please — wards of the Government who had revolted against its authority, and were fighting mercilessly and neither giving nor expect ing quarter. I then thought that captives taken in the future should be executed at once, and upon the spot, as the surest and speediest method of settling the Modoc problem.

QUESTION — You deemed them directly amenable to a military edict?
ANSWER — When captured while fighting against the military forces of the United States and as a separate nation or tribe I was disposed to deal with them accordingly. Since the capture I have ascertained that the

[1] Brevet Major General, U.S. Army, and Colonel, Twenty Third Inf. Reg.

authorities of Jackson County, Oregon, have found indictments against certain members of the band but I have not deemed it proper to turn them over to the Civil Courts, because they were waging war against the Government at the time the murders upon which the indictments were found, and also for the reason that after the capture they were prisoners of the Government and not directly answerable to civil laws.

During my command here I have observed that the citizens desiring protection for person and property, or indemnification for loss, invariably appeal to the authority of the United States; but now that the war is over and the murderers are captives, both the public and the local authorities want to take the punishment of the offenders into their own hands.

The threats of the people and the recent bloody act in this neighborhood, when four old and defenseless male captives en route from Fairchild's ranch to the camp, were murdered by civilians, indicate to me that a trial by civil law would be a useless farce. The people have made up their minds that the prisoners are guilty.

QUESTION — How about the military commission?

ANSWER — It is suggested that a military commission will be ordered to try the criminals. If the idea is carried out, the officers composing the court should be of high rank, and men who have had no immediate connection with the Modoc difficulty.

QUESTION — Matters are so mixed that it would take a long while to dispose of the case?

ANSWER — Such a Commission would probably try each case separately, and require about six months to perform the work, to say nothing of the expense involved upon such a proceeding. I thought to avoid an unnnecessary expense and the farce of a trial by doing the work myself.

Owing to the dilatory manner in which the Modocs were treated by those in charge in the beginning of these difficulties, the Indians obtained a fearful advantage over us and slaughtered so many people that the country was astonished, even shocked, and now I fear that they will get the advantage in the closing scenes. This same fear is disturbing the minds of the citizens of the frontier. Justice it seems to me has already been very tardy in coming and is approaching from so many different directions, and in such questionable shape and garbs, that I doubt her success in meeting the requirements of the case.

QUESTION — What is the Indian's idea of justice?

ANSWER — The Indians do not recognize the jurisdic tion of civil or military courts, because they are incapable of comprehending the workings of either. These Modocs cannot understand what is meant by a court. They have been interrogated on this subject. They would regard a Court trial with its technicalities, its testimony, etc., as a kind of jugglery, and if convicted and sentenced to death could not be made to understand that justice figured in the business at all.

QUESTION — Might is right with them, is it?

ANSWER — Yes, in a measure. That is so. They they have committed deeds and merit death, and in fact the real murderers have daily expected to be hanged. They believe the military has the power and the right to inflict the punishment of death.

QUESTION — Have not the prisoners to be sorted out?

ANSWER — Yes, in a measure. That is so. They believe that respect. The murders and arrests occurred in Oregon and California, and are badly mixed; my proposed course settled this question. By a single stroke the Gordeon (sic) knot was to be cut.

SUGGESTION — The proposition was a humane one.

ANSWER — I honestly believe it was on account of the prospects of the Indians. They are cooped up in tents, men, women, and children — guilty and innocent —

fearing massacre all the time, and must remain in this condition of suspense for months to come.

QUESTION — You had a choice assortment of juniper limbs for scaffold material?

ANSWER — I had procured lumber, chains, rope, tackles and all other phariphernalia (sic) of an execution, and selected Friday last as doomsday [June 6th].

— The Charges Against Jack —

Thursday forenoon I drew up this declaration of charges to read to Jack later in the day:

HEADQUARTERS DEPT. OF COLUMBIA, IN THE FIELD, TULE LAKE, Cal., June [5th], 1873. — Jack: Since the white man first began to travel through or settle in the (country) occupied by the Modoc people, of which you claim to be one of the chiefs, the Modocs have been known as a band of merciless robbers and murderers. The history of your tribe is filled with murders of the white race, and even among your Indian neighbors you are known as a domineering and tyrannical tribe.

Old settlers in the country report as many as three hundred murders committed by your people within the limits of the present generation. Along the shores of this beautiful little lake, in view of which we now stand, are the graves of over sixty victims of Modoc barbarity, all murdered by your immediate ancestors in one brutal act. They were peaceful emigrants — men, women, and children passing quietly through the country on the public highway. For these many crimes no adequate punishment has ever been visited upon the guilty parties either as a tribe or individually.

On the contrary the Government has tacitly over- looked them. A few years ago regardless of these acts of treachery it gave your tribe a reservation of that land for a home, where if you chose you could remain and enjoy the annual bounties of the government unmolested. You all went upon the reservation thus provided, and a part of your tribe has remained, but you and your band seem to have preferred the war path. You left the reservation; you spurned the kindness of the Government and even resisted the soldiers in the execution of their duty to force you back to the reservation.

You hastened to war, and emulating the bloody deeds of your fathers you again strewd the shores of Tule Lake with the slain victims of your bloody band. All these victims were peaceful citizens, unsuspectingly slaughtered while at their daily avocations. You then fled to your stronghold in the Lava Bed, prepared for war, and defied the power of the government. Still the President at Washington ordered the soldiers to desist until the Peace Commissioners could have a talk with you and if possible avoid the shedding of more blood. Their efforts were fruitless.

After much delay and many attempts at conciliation on their part you decoyed the Commissioners into your hands and murdered them. You have murdered every soldier who has fallen into your hands, armed or unarmed. These acts have placed you and your band outside the rules of civilized warfare; in other words, you have made yourselves outlaws. As such, since my arrival here as the successor of General Canby, whom you murdered with your own hands, I have made unremitting war upon you, until at last you have been captured, after much expense to the Government and the loss of many valuable lives.

Now that I have recounted to you the history of your tribe and recent acts of yourself and band, I will close this interview by informing you that I have this day directed that you and the following named confederates and members of your band, be executed at sunset to-morrow in the presence of the troops paraded for that purpose, your people and the assembled citizens of the country.

(Blank space for names)

ORDER COUNTERMANDED

General Davis continued: While I was preparing a list

of those I intended to execute, a courier arrived with
instructions from Washington to hold the prisoners until
further orders.

QUESTION — What movement did you propose making
after the execution?

ANSWER — I intended organizing a force for the
purpose and starting for the Columbia, probably for
Lapwai, seeing and talking with as many chiefs as
possible while en route. I knew that the prompt execution
of the Modoc outlaws would facilitate peace talks among
the Indians of Oregon and Washington Territory as well
as California, and have the tendency to quiet the Indians
all through the country. The Indians all know that we
have captured the Modocs, and they will quickly learn
the news, if the death penalty is inflicted. The achieve-
ment would result in mutual benefits to both indians and
whites. With the prestige the troops have gained we could
do great good by such a campaign.

And so closed the interview.

BOGUS CHARLEY.

I certify that L. HELLER has this day taken the Photographs of the above
Modoc Indian, prisoner under my charge.
    Capt. C. B. THROCKMORTON, 4th U. S. Artillery, Officer of the Day.
I am cognizant of the above fact.   GEN. JEFF. C. DAVIS, U. S. A.

Photo no. 50. Bogus Charley, Modoc Indian. One of the four "Blood-hounds". Landrum Collection.

HOOKA JIM.

I certify that L. **Heller** has this day taken the Photographs of the above Modoc Indian, prisoner under my charge.
Capt. C. B. **Throckmorton**, 4th U. S. Artillery, Officer of the Day.
I am cognizant of the above fact. **Gen. Jeff. C. Davis**, U. S. A.

Photo no. 55. Hooker (Hooka) Jim, Modoc Indian. One of the four "Blood-hounds". Landrum Collection.

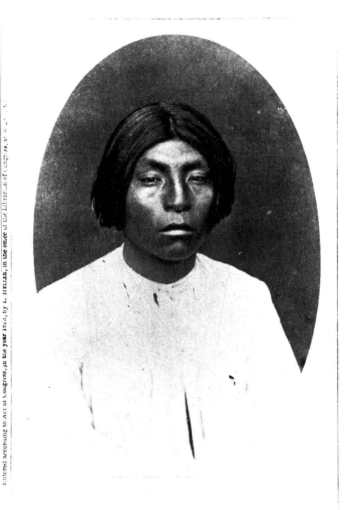

SHACKNASTY JIM.

I certify that L. HELLER has this day taken the Photographs of the above Modoc Indian, prisoner under my charge.
Capt. C. B. THROCKMORTON, 4th U. S. Artillery, Officer of the Day.
I am cognizant of the above fact. GEN. JEFF. C. DAVIS, U. S. A.

Photo no. 60. Shacknasty Jim, Modoc Indian. One of the four "Bloodhounds". His brothers, Ellen's Man George and Shacknasty Frank were killed in the Modoc Indian War. Landrum Collection.

STEAMBOAT FRANK.

I certify that L. HELLER has this day taken the Photographs of the above Modoc Indian, prisoner under my charge.
Capt. C. B. THROCKMORTON, 4th U. S. Artillery, Officer of the Day.
I am cognizant of the above fact. GEN. JEFF. C. DAVIS, U. S. A

Photo no. 65. Steamboat Frank, Modoc Indian. One of the four "Bloodhounds". In later years became Frank Modoc, ordained minister. Landrum Collection.

Photo no. 70. Bvt. Maj. Gen. Jefferson C. Davis, Col. 23rd Infantry. Became commanding general of the Dept. of Columbia after Canby's death. Landrum Collection.

Photo no. 80. Fort Klamath, Oregon; 1863-1890. Infantry barracks at left; cavalry barracks at right; guard house is to right of the latter. Landrum Collection.

OLD FORT KLAMATH ORE.

Photo no. 85. Fort Klamath. Commanding officer's quarters. Fisher Collection.

Photo no. 90. Fort Klamath. Guard house, site of the confinement of the
Modoc Indian prisoners. Landrum Collection.

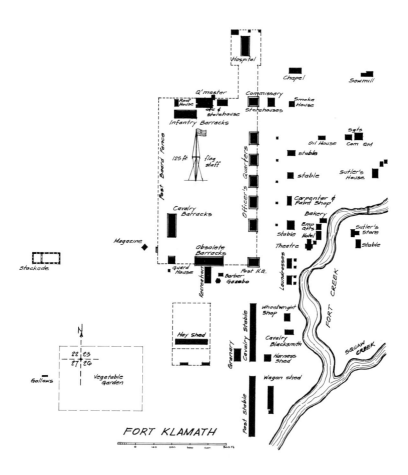

Hospital

Chapel

Sawmill

Q'master

Commissary

Smoke House

Post House

QM & Storehouse

Storehouses

Infantry Barracks

Sgts

Oil House

Corn QM

stable

Post Board Fence

125 ft flag staff

Officer's Quarters

stable

Sutler's House

Cavalry Barracks

Carpenter & Paint Shop

Bakery

Emp aths Hotel

Sutler's Store

Magazine

Obsolete Barracks

stable

stable

Theatre

Stockade

Guard House

Recreation

Post H.Q.

Barber

Gazebo

Laundresses

FORT CREEK

Wheelwright Shop

N

Hay Shed

Cavalry Stable

Cavalry Blacksmith

SQUAW CREEK

22 | 23
―――
27 | 26

Granary

Harness Shed

Gallows

Vegetable Garden

Wagon shed

Post Stable

FORT KLAMATH

0   100   200   300   400   500 ft

Map II

Photo no. 100. Lieut. Col. Washington L. Elliott, 1st Cavalry. President of the military commission. Landrum Collection.

Photo no. 105. Capt. Henry C. Hasbrouck, Battery B, 4th Artillery. Commanded escort taking Modoc Indian exiles to Fort D. A. Russell. Photo taken when he was the commandant of cadets at West Point. Courtesy U. S. Military Academy Library. Landrum Collection.

Photo no. 110. Fort Klamath. Adjutant's office, site of the trial of the Modoc Indian prisoners. Fisher Collection.

Photo no. 115. Elisha Steele. One time Indian agent for the Siskiyou area. Friend and confidante of the Modoc Indians. Wilbur Crim Collection.

SCHONCHIN AND JACK.

I certify that L. HELLER has this day taken the Photographs of the above Modoc Indians, prisoners under my charge.
Capt. C. B. THROCKMORTON, 4th U. S. Artillery, Officer of the Day.
I am cognizant of the above fact.   GEN. JEFF. C. DAVIS, U. S. A.

Published by WATKINS. Yosemite Art Gallery, 22 & 26 Montgomery St., opp. Lick House.

Photo no. 125. Schonchin and Captain Jack, Modoc Indians. Lava Beds National Monument Collection.

LOST RIVER MURDERERS.

I certify that L. HELLER has this day taken the Photographs of the above Modoc Indians, prisoners under my charge.
Capt. C. B. THROCKMORTON, 4th U. S. Artillery, Officer of the Day.
I am cognizant of the above fact.   GEN. JEFF. C. DAVIS, U. S. A.

Photo no. 130. Lost River Murderers, Modoc Indians. Left is Curly-Haired Jack. Other two unknown. Landrum Collection.

LOST RIVER MURDERERS.

I certify that L. HELLER has this day taken the Photographs of the above Modoc Indians, prisoners under my charge.
Capt. C. B. THROCKMORTON, 4th U. S. Artillery, Officer of the Day.
I am cognizant of the above fact. GEN. JEFF. C. DAVIS, U. S. A.

Photo no. 135. Lost River Murderers, Modoc Indians. Left is Curly-headed Doctor; center is William, the Wild Gal's Man. Right, unknown. Landrum Collection.

CHAPTER 5

BY NORTH to FORT KLAMATH

(Dispatch)

Report of Inspection of Public Buildings at Fort Klamath, Oregon by Captain Robert Pollock, 21st Infantry, A. A. Q. M., June 30, 1873. [EXTRACT]......
Guard House

Class 5. Dimensions 32 x 32 ft. 10 ft in height, divided into four parts. Guard Room 18 x 31 ft. Large Cell for general prisoners 12 x 15 ft. Three Cells (for prisoners in close confinement) Two of which is 5 x 12 ft. in clear, and One 8 x 12 ft in the clear. Ventilation of the small cells very limited. The Porch Roof extends over the front 7 ft 6 in. This building is constructed of logs, hewn 6 inches square, and in good repair......

Buildings constructed during the year ending June 30" 1873.......
...One (1) porch in front of Guard House. There was also erected in center of Parade Ground a Flag-staff 125 ft. high....

Remarks

There are but two wagon roads leading from this post. One of which runs in a South-westerly direction, crossed the mountains 20 miles from the Post, and leads into and through the Rogue River Valley to Jacksonville. Jackson county Oregon. Distance from Post 98 miles. This road is open only during the months of July August, September, and October, and is completely blocked by snow during the remainder of the year The other road leads in a

South-easterly direction along the banks of Klamath
Lake, to Linkville Oregon thence across the mountains,
and down Bear-river valley in the direction of Jacksonville Oregon. Distance 120 miles. This road is open all the
year. The nearest Post Office is Linkville, Jackson Co.,
Oregon, from which place the mail for the post is brought
once a week by Military Express.

Rob Pollock
Capt. 21st Infantry
A. A. Q. M.

(Dispatch)

Letter from Fort Klamath

Fort Klamath — The Modoc Captives — Their Fourth (sic)
coming trial   — The Stockade — Modoc Harmony —
Chosen Victims — Officers of the Post, &c.   Correspond-
ence of the Bellows Falls Times.

FORT KLAMATH, Oregon
July 5th, 1873

Fort Klamath is justly reputed one of the prettiest and
most attractive military posts on the Pacific coast and
certainly is a grand place for the closing scenes in the
Modoc drama — evidently now so near at hand.

The post is located on the east side of a broad green
meadow, belted by lofty pines which in turn is surrounded by snowy peaks comprising a portion of the Cascade
range. A carpet of green with a forest border and a fringe
of mountains, running rivulets of most beautiful cristal
(sic) water, whitened cottages, neat barracks, comfortable
stables and commodious storehouses and offices, with a
great many tents for present necessity and forming a
pleasant contrast, the whole constituting a landscape
beautiful to behold, harmonious in its various phases and
impressive in its character.

Such is Fort Klamath, the place selected from which
justice is to be meted out to the erring Modocs. Its
latitude is 42 degrees 41 minutes north, longitude 40

degrees 44 minutes west (sic; this longitude is some 4 degrees in error - about 250 miles; note that it is called from the Washington meridian - not Greenwich) and altitude 4200 feet above the level of the sea. It was established in 1863 and was built to accommodate one company of cavalry and one company of infantry.

The buildings comprising the post are in good repair, consisting of officers' quarters, barracks, hospital, storehouses, guard house, magazine, offices, and large and well appointed stables. The officers' quarters, barracks, hospital and storehouses have a frontage on a beautiful parade ground, in the center of which, from a staff of beautiful symmetrical proportions floats the proud emblem of our country's freedom.

The officers' quarters are neat, cheerful and convenient. Here one finds, even in the bachelor homes the refinements of civilization, articles of virtue, objets d'art, and other relics of gentility which serve to remind one of brighter days when associated with the eclat of social centers and had engagements with goddesses fully as fickle and potent as Old Mars.

— THE STOCKADE —

Adjacent to the Post and in the corner of the camp of the battalion of the 12th infantry comprising companies "E", and "G" commanded by Lieuts. Camp and Kingsbury, is a stockade of pine logs, wherein most of the Modoc prisoners are confined. The stockade is one hundred and fifty feet long by fifty wide and eleven feet high. It is divided into two sections the larger being 100 x 50 feet the smaller 50 x 50 feet. The logs reach four feet below the surface and are thoroughly tamped and on the outside near the top are cleated together rendering the structure compact and durable.

Each section has its own door. The necessity for dividing the stockade arises from the fact that the Cottonwood and Lost River factions of the tribe cannot agree together and ache to engage in a war of extermination among themselves.

The stockade is guarded by twenty men, five of whom are always on duty. Guards pace to and fro in front of the doors and along raised platforms at the corners of the stockade. No one enters the stockade without permission from the officer on duty. No Modoc passes out except under guard and in the case of a warrior two guards are detailed to accompany him until his return. The guards not immediately on post are quartered in tents at one corner of the stockade, while companies E and G, 12th infantry are encamped just to the north of the stockade. Troops comprising the regular garrison are in barracks two hundred yards to the east of the stockade. Hasbrouck's mounted battery "B", 4th artillery are encamped about one half a mile to the west of the stockade.

In addition to the officers on duty, Lieuts. Camp or Kingsbury are always present in the camp of their battalion ready for any emergency. Thus it will be observed that our pets are well guarded and cared for, in case an attempt should be made to escape. I should have also remarked that a portion of Hasbrouck's battery is constantly mounted and ready for immediate use.

Rations are issued to the Modocs every morning, and they are allowed to cook the same to suit themselves inside the stockade. Wood is furnished for that purpose. But they chafe under restraint and those who can speak a little English inquire anxiously when they will be given their liberty. They are generally of the opinion that Captain Jack, Schonchin, and some of the other leaders will be severely punished and that the remainder will be sent to San Francisco and confined on a little island.

— MODOC HARMONY —

The harmony existing in these Modoc families is wonderful to behold. Never have I seen its equal in any other country or among any other people. The woman has things her own way all the time. She can get up first in the morning, build the fire, clean up the premises, bring all the rations from the commissary, bring the wood and water with which she cooks breakfast, do the cooking, wrap the rags about the children, and never be interfered with once. The male Modoc never gets under foot. He remains under the blankets until he is satisfied the "muck-a-muck" is ready, and then he comes forth and eats. He seldom if ever trifles or interferes with the domestic arrangements of the family as long as he gets enough to eat.

— CHOSEN VICTIMS —

Eleven of the Modocs occupy three secure cells on the ground floor of the Post Guard house, viz., Captain Jack, Schonchin, Boston Charley, Black Jim, Curly-headed Doctor, Curly-headed Doctor's son, Dave, One-eyed Mose, Pete, Barncho, and Sloluck; everyone of these are in heavy shackles, and some of them are shackled in pairs for greater security.

The Guard house is a white building about 40 feet square, — of pleasant exterior, built of logs about one foot square laid horizontal and close together. In front is a porch which adds to the comeliness of the building and gives it the air of comfort. The building is whitewashed inside and out.

The cells in which the prisoners are confined are rooms 7 x 9 feet with grating for light and air a short distance from the ceiling. The partitions between the cells are of heavy plank and very strong. The doors open into the main guard room and are holeless. The prisoners can hear little and see less, and nothing transpiring outside of their respective cells is visible to them. They are only taken out twice each day while their shackles are carefully examined by the officers of the day.

The prisoners look bad, and wear a dejected look.; this close confinement is killing them by inches, and they look as if death in any form would be welcomed as a measure of relief. Two or three times each week they are taken out of the guardhouse and marched under a strong guard over to the stockade and allowed to see their families. Three months of such close confinement will kill the entire number.

— OFFICERS OF THE POST —

The officers on duty here are:

Captain Henry C. Hasbouck, 4th Artillery, Commanding Light Battery "B" and Post;

Captain Robert Pollock, 21st Infantry, Commanding Company "F";

First Lieutenant James B. Hazelton, 4th Artillery and Battery "B";

First Lieutenant Erskine M. Camp, 12th Infantry, Commanding Company "G";

First Lieutenant Matthew C. Grier, 4th Artillery, A.A.Q.M. and A.C.S.;

First Lieutenant Sydney W. Taylor, 4th Artillery, Battery "B";

First Lieutenant Harry R. Anderson, 4th Artillery and Battery "B";

Second Lieutenant George W. Kingsbury, 12th Infantry, Commanding Company "E", and Post Adjutant;

Assistant Surgeon Henry McElderry, Post Surgeon;

Acting Assistant Surgeon John Tallon, Assistant Post Surgeon;

The Command consists of Light Battery "B", 4th Artillery, Companies "E" and "G", 12th Infantry, and Company "F", 21st Infantry; The trial of Captain Jack and other murderous Modocs, contrary to general expectation in this mixed community, bids fair to have a speedy beginning, and as a natural consequence there is rejoicing among officers, soldiers, and captives. The last week has been a tedious one. But the future looks bright and promising for every one save those whose fates are involved in the trial. What with the sessions of the Commission, the influx of witnesses and visitors, and the probabilities of slight social sensations, we are likely to be kept awake during the daytime without exertion.

Speaking of visitors, reminds me that the furore over Captain Jack, has been prolific of funny incidents.

Women and children, to say nothing of the crowds of men, have made long journeys on horseback just to get a peep at the Chief, and have trembled, when asking his whereabouts, lest they should be told he was no more.

One venerable farmer of Oregon, came prepared to pay for his share of the show, bringing from his Web-foot home a barrel of cider, and was surprised to learn that admission was free. He saw Jack, sold his cider, and departed for home a richer and a happier man.

Another chap, a long, lean fellow with a cork leg, told me he had travelled a long distance, over rough roads, to see the Modocs, and trusted that he had not made a fruitless journey. The sad cadence of his voice and his solicitude presented a specimen of grim humor that was funny to a laughable degree. The party with the game leg was allowed to feast his eyes on Jack. And so it goes.

July 5, 1873

— CONDITION OF THE CAPTIVES —

There is sickness among the prisoners in the guard-house, and in less than three months we shall hear of deaths by disease in that locality. Captain Jack and the Curly-headed Doctor are getting gaunt and weak by reason of close confinement. Lack of fresh air will soon begin to wear away others of the band. B (Bunker? Bogart?)

CHAPTER 6

MILITARY JURISPRUDENCE

(Letter)

HEADQUARTERS DEPARTMENT OF THE COLUMBIA
Fort Klamath, OGN, June 30, 1873
Major Herbert P. Curtis
Judge Advocate of Military Commission

Dear Sir:

I have the honor herewith, to enclose you a copy of the order convening a Military Commission for the trial of the Indian Captives known as Captain Jack's Modoc Tribe. These Indians are accused of committing crimes while engaged in War with the United States Government in violation of the rules of honorable warfare. They are accused of murdering peaceful citizens who were non-combatants, of murdering officials of the government while holding a peace commission under a flag of truce between the hostile lines, and also of killing wounded soldiers whom the accidents of War threw into their hands.

By reference to the enclosed Copy of an opinion of the Attorney General of the United States, recently given with special reference to the case of these captives — You will perceive that they may be tried by a Military Commission.

You will proceed to the trial of the accused parties and bring them before the commission under such charges and specifications as in your judgment will be sustained by the evidence. A list containing the names of the accused parties is respectfully submitted; it contains all the able-bodied men of the Band now in Custody.

Very respectfully
Your obedient Servant

(Signed) Jeff C Davis.
Brevet Major General
Commanding.

• • •

(1st enclosure)   (Letter)
                         DEPARTMENT OF JUSTICE,
                         July 7, 1873

To the PRESIDENT:
SIR: I have the honor to acknowledge the receipt from you of several papers relative to the Modoc Indians now in custody of the United States Army, with a request for my opinion as to the authority to try certain of the prisoners by a military tribunal...

...(Excerpts)... Military jurisdiction is of two kinds: First, that which is conferred and defined by statute; second, that which is derived from the common law of war. Military offenses, under the statute law, must be tried in the manner therein directed, but military offenses, which do not come within the statute, must be tried and punished under the common law of war. The character of the courts which exercise these jurisdictions depends upon the local laws of each particular country.

In the Armies of the United States the first is exercised by courts-martial, while cases which do not come within the "Rules and Articles of War," or the jurisdiction conferred by statute on courts-martial, are tried by military commissions. All the authorities which I have been able to examine upon this subject harmonize with these "instructions".

According to the laws of war there is nothing more sacred than a flag of truce dispatched in good faith, and there can be no greater act of perfidy and treachery than the assassination of its bearers after they have been acknowledged and received by those to whom they are sent. No statute of the United States makes this act a crime, and therefore it is not punishable under the "Rules and Articles of War," and if punishable at all, it must be through a power derived from the usages of war... ...All the proceedings in (cases of this kind) derive their authority and validity from the common law of war. Certain persons, it will be remembered, were tried and convicted in the same way for the assassination of President Lincoln.

... Attorney-General Speed, in discussing this subject, (Opinions, vol 11, 297,) says: We have seen that when war comes the laws and usages of war come also, and that during the war they are a part of the laws of the land. Under the Constitution, Congress may define and punish offenses against those laws, but in default of Congress defining those laws and prescribing a punishment for their infraction, and the mode of proceeding to ascertain whether an offense has been committed and what punishement is to be inflicted, the Army must be governed by the laws and usages of war as understood and practices by the civilized nations of the world.

Again:...

If the prisoner be a regular unoffending soldier of the opposing party to the war, he should be treated with all the courtesy and kindness consistent with his safe custody; if he has offended against the laws of war, he should have such trial, and be punished as the laws of war require... A bushwhacker, a jayhawker, a bandit, a war rebel, an assassin, being public enemies, may be tried, condemned, and executed as offenders against the laws of war...

...According to the "Instructions" heretofore referred to, no civil tribunal has jurisdiction in the case disclosed by the papers before me. Sections 40 and 41 thereof are as follows:

> 40. There exists no law or body of authoritative rules of action between hostile armies except that branch of the law of nature and nations which is called the law and usages of war on land.
>
> 41. All municipal law of the ground on

which the armies stand, or of the countries to which they belong, is silent and of no effect between armies in the field.

Manifestly, these rules, to a great extent, if not altogether, are correct; for it cannot be pretended that a United States soldier is guilty of murder if he kills a public enemy in battle, which would be the case if the municipal law was in force and applicable to an act committed under such circumstances.

All the laws and customs of civilized warfare may not be applicable to an armed conflict with the Indian tribes upon our western frontier, but the circumstances attending the assassination of Canby and Thomas are such as to make their murder as much a violation of the laws of savage as of civilized warfare; and the Indian concerned it fully understood the baseness and treachery of their act.

It is difficult to define exactly the relations of the Indian tribes of the United States; but as they have been recognized as independent communities for treaty-making purposes, and as they frequently carry on organized and protracted wars, they may properly, as it seems to me, be held subject to those rules of warfare which make a negotiation for peace after hostilities possible, and which make perfidy like that in question punishable by military authority.

Doubtless the war with the Modocs is practically ended, unless some of them should escape and renew hostilities. But it is the right of the United States, as there is no agreement for peace, to determine for themselves whether or not anything more ought to be done for the protection of the country or the punishment of crimes growing out of the war. Section 59 of said "Instructions" is as follows:

> 59. A prisoner of war remains answerable for his crimes committed against the captor's army or people, committed before he was captured, and for which he has not been punished by his own authorities.

My conclusion, therefore, is that a military commission may be appointed to try such of the Modoc Indians now in custody as are charged with offenses against the recognized laws of war, and that if upon such trial any are found guilty, they may be subjected to such punishment as those laws require or justify.

Very respectfully, your obedient servant,

GEO. H. WILLIAMS
Attorney-General

• • •

(Telegram)

HEADQUARTERS ARMY of the UNITED STATES
Washington, D. C., June 7, 1873

Attorney-General decides that the acts of the Modoc Indians subsequent to their first resistance, when required to return to their reservation, constituted war in a technical sense; that crimes afterward committed against the laws of war are triable and punishable by military courts, preferably military commission.

You may order the commmission to be governed by all the rules and conditions familiar to you in 1864, and meantime I will send by mail the opinion at length of the Attorney-General.

W. T. SHERMAN,
General.

Gen. J. M. SCHOFIELD,
Commanding Division, San Francisco

• • •

(Telegram)

WEST POINT, N. Y., June 11, 1873

General Sherman directs me to transmit the following

order for your action:

> WM. D. WHIPPLE,
> Assistant Adjutant-General

Gen. J. M. SCHOFIELD,
San Francisco, Cal.

● ● ●

(Letter)

> WEST POINT, N. Y., June 11, 1873

I am instructed by the President to direct you to instruct General Schofield to have the Modoc prisoners tried by military commission, the proceedings of said commission to be sent to the President for approval.

> Very respectfully, &c.,
> WM. W. BELKNAP,
> Secretary of War.

GENERAL SHERMAN,
West Point, N.Y.

● ● ●

(Letter)

> SAN FRANCISCO, June 12, 1873

GENERAL W. T. SHERMAN, Washington, D. C.:

The order of the President regarding proceeding of commission has been sent to General Davis.

Agreeably to your telegram eighth (seventh?) instant, General Davis was informed that Modoc prisoners would be tried by military commissions, and that as the commander of department and troops in the field, he had, under act of July 2, 1864, full power and authority to appoint the commission and order the execution of the sentences in these cases. He was informed that the sentence of the commission must be governed by the usages and laws of war, and that he had the discretion to exempt from capital punishment those whose services entitled them to mercy. I send you this information, thinking and hoping you may request the President to modify his order. The prisoners will be tried under the act referred to for the crime of murder and as accessories thereto.

General Davis desires Major Curtis to report to him as judge advocate of commission. The trial he says will take place at Fort Klamath, to which post prisoners are now en route.

J. M. SCHOFIELD.
Major-General

• • •

(Telegram)
WEST POINT, (June?) 16, 1873

Gen. W. T. SHERMAN:

President say (sic) he does not think it best to modify the order.

WM. W. BELKNAP,
Secretary of War

• • •

(Telegram)

WAR DEPARTMENT, ADJUTANT-GENERAL'S OFFICE,
Washington, June 30, 1873

The Secretary of War instructs me to inform you that by direction of the President, you will cause no cases whatsoever, to be brought before the Military Commission except those of the murderers of the three Officers assassinated by "Captain Jack" and his immediate associates; the three officers being General Canby, Doctor Thomas and Lieutenant Sherwood. And further, to hold in military custody all the other captured Indians as prisoners of war, to be disposed of hereafter as circumstances may warrant.

Acknowledge receipt.

E. D. TOWNSEND,
Adjutant General

Maj. Gen. J. M. SCHOFIELD,
San Francisco, California.

• • •

(Dispatch)
— **THE MILITARY COMMISSION** —

The order convening the Military Commission for the trial of the Modoc prisoners has been published as follows:

HEADQUARTERS DEPARTMENT OF THE COLUMBIA IN THE FIELD
Fort Klamath, Oregon, June 30, 1873

Special Field Orders. No. 1
(Extract) — A Military Commission is hereby appointed to meet at Fort Klamath, Oregon, on Tuesday, July 1st, 1873, at ten o'clock a.m. or as soon thereafter as practicable for the trial of the Modoc chief known as Captain Jack, and such other Indian captives as may be properly brought before it.

(Detail for the Commission)

Lieut. Col. Wash[ington] L. Elliott, First Cavalry; Capt. John Mendenhall, Fourth Artillery; Capt. Henry C. Hasbrouck, Fourth Artillery; Capt. Robert Pollock, Twenty First Infantry; Second Lieut. George W. Kingsbury,

Twelfth Infantry; Maj. Herbert P. Curtis, Judge Advocate
of U.S.A, Judge Advocate of the Commission. No other
officers than those named can be assembled without
manifest injury to the service. Should any of the officers
named in the order be unable to attend, the commission
will nevertheless proceed to and continue the business
before it, provided the number present be not less than
the minimum prescribed by law.

> (Signed) J. C. Davis,
> Brevet Maj. Gen
> Commanding

(Dispatch)

— DAILY EVENING BULLETIN —
[San Francisco]

SATURDAY EVENING, JULY 5, 1873

THE MODOC TRIALS
The Military Commission
SKETCH OF THE MEMBERS
[FROM OUR SPECIAL CORRESPONDENT]

FORT KLAMATH, July 1st — A. M.

— THE MEN WHO TRY THE MODOCS —
The officers selected by General Davis to try the
Modocs are all excellent men, and are the better for the
duty, I believe, because they are not men of the highest
rank. They all stand well in the army, are anxious to
mete out exact justice, and will zealously perform the
work for which they have been chosen. The men of the
Commission I give below.

— LIEUTENANT-COLONEL WASHINGTON L. ELLIOTT —
The senior member of the Commission, Lieutenant-
Colonel Washington L. Elliott, entered the regular army
May 27, 1846, having been appointed from Pennsylva-
nia... ...Colonel Elliott has been stationed at Benicia

Barracks of late, and was not engaged in the Modoc difficulties, but his record and reputation are of the highest order. He is about fifty years of age, though easily taken for forty, and is admirably adapted for the senior position of the Commission.

— CAPTAIN JOHN MENDENHALL —

Captain John Mendenhall, of Battery G, Fourth Artillery, senior Captain of the Fourth Regiment, and more familiarly known as Colonel Mendenhall, was appointed to West Point from Indiana in 1847, and graduating in 1851, was brevetted Second Lieutenant in the First Dragoons... ...after the battle of Stone River the Captain was made Judge Advocate of the Twenty-first Army Corps... ...He was ordered to Black Point, San Francisco, in November, 1872, and in April, 1873, came to the scene of the Modoc troubles. Captain Mendenhall is of light complexion, stands about five feet 9 inches in the hob-nailed shoes worn on this expedition, and weighs at a guess one hundred and forty five pounds. His hair and whiskers are intermingled with grey. His grey eyes are bright and twinkling and his face is a pleasant one. He is on the sunny side of forty-four. He is deservedly popular in the army, is a man of sound judgement, and one who can always be relied upon. The large and varied experience of this gentleman has qualified him for the position, and there is no doubt but his calm, cool judgement will cause him to do exact justice to the parties concerned.

— CAPTAIN HENRY C. HASBROUCK —

Captain Henry C. Hasbrouck, of Battery B, Fourth Artillery, entered West Point from Newberg, New York, in 1856, graduated in 1861, and was immediately made Second Lieutenant of the West Point Battery and stationed at Washington...

...He came here an utter stranger to Indian warfare, with a Battery unused to small arms, and really thought to be placed in the shade by veterans in the business; but instead of taking a few straggling laurels, he carried off a

whole wreath. His famous ten days' scout, which resulted
in the defeat of the Modocs at Dry Lake, the disaffection
among the braves, the separation, and ultimately the
surrender at Fairchild's Ranch, was one of the greatest
achievements of the war...

...Captain Hasbrouck is a handsome, dashing officer of
thirty-three, has a fine soldierly bearing, wears a martial
moustache and no beard, stands about five feet ten
inches, and weighs about one hundred and fifty-five
pounds. He is the man one would naturally pick out for
the leader of a forlorn hope — a wide-awake, energetic
man, brimful of vim. He is a good man for the
Commission, because, don't you see, he has had his
satisfaction of the Modocs, and can now judge the
criminals in a critical though impartial manner, and then
he is as honest as the day is long. If he had a wife, people
might sympathize with him for being compelled to
remain on the frontier, but as he is modest and single, it
is about the best thing he can do.

— CAPTAIN ROBERT POLLOCK —

In 1846 Captain Pollock, always called Colonel outside
of papers in tape, was commissioned Second Lieutenant of
a Virginia regiment and sent to the Mexican war. He
served with the army of occupation, under General
Taylor, to the close of the contest, when he was mustered
out of the service with the balance of the volunteers. He
came to California as a citizen, in 1854, and he has never
since been east of the Rocky Mountains...

...He is now Captain of Company D, Twenty-first
Infantry, and his proper station is Camp Warner. Captain
Pollock is a man who will pull down the scales at two
hundred without the slightest exertion — a sturdy,
compact man, with the bluff though genial manners of a
ship captain. He has a large and interesting family of
children, merry little girls, who are the rays of sunshine
at the post. He has an excellent reputation as an officer,
is thoroughly acquainted with Indian character, and
will do his duty in the Modoc case. He is on the shady
side of forty-five. San Francisco is largely indebted to

him for the organization of that crack military company, the National Guard.

— LIEUTENANT GEORGE W. KINGSBURY —

The appointment of Second Lieutenant George W. Kingsbury as a member of the Commission is a handsome compliment to a gallant soldier and an accomplished gentleman. Lieutenant Kingsbury enlisted as a private soldier in the Sixteenth Regiment of Vermont Volunteers in 1862...

...He was afterward transferred to the Twelfth Infantry, and in February, 1870, was assigned to duty at Camp Gaston, Cal., where he acted as Post Adjutant, Quarter-master, and Commissary until the Modoc troubles came. After Colonel Wright's death, Lieutenant Kingsbury assumed charge of Company E, Twelfth Infantry, and retains the command.

Though little less than thirty-three years of age, he is thoroughly grounded in military matters, and upon the legal questions arising during the trial his advice will be of value. Lieutenant Kingbury has been Judge Advocate of the Court-Martial held in the field under General Davis' orders. He is by no means a novice in military law. He is a trim, light complexioned benedict, and will kick the beam at one hundred and twenty-five pounds. He is the junior member of the Commission.

— MAJOR HERBERT P. CURTIS —
JUDGE-ADVOCATE

Major Herbert P. Curtis, Judge-Advocate of the court, entered the Fifth Massachusetts Cavalry in January, 1862, served in the Army of the Potomac until June, 1865, and was then summoned to Washington and made Judge Advocate with the rank of Major. He has entered upon his work with a hearty good will, and will undoubtedly do his level best to straighten out one of the worst legal tangles in existence. There cannot be convictions without evidence — and evidence, except in the Peace Commission tragedy, is a scarce article.

• • •

(Letter)

Fort Jones, Cal.
July 1st 1873

To Lieut Col. Elliot, Capt Mendenhall — Capt Hasbrouck,
Capt Pollock — Major Curtis and Lieut Kingsbury.

Members of the Court Marshall (sic) convened to try
the Modoc Captives

Gentlemen—

Have you the authority to
investigate the cause of the late war with the Modocs.? If
so, I desire to be present, at such investigation — As I
feel a deep interest in the matter — A great many
valuable lives have been sacrificed. Justice demands
that the instigators of the war should be brought to
justice. If the Military must do the fighting — I think
that it is about time to remove all dishonest agents and
speculators from the reservations — and let the Military
department take charge of the Indian Department, and
then we will have peace and fair dealing with the
Government and the Indians -

Gentlemen — I do not propose
to suggest or influence your action, but humanity
demands a thorough investigation of the causes of the
late war — and in case you have the authority to extend
your investigation beyond the Assassination and Murder
of the Peace Commissioners. I desire to be present at
such investigation with such evidence as I have been
able to collect, much of which — I think — will convince
the public that fraud and speculation was the cause of
the war — and will I hope have some weight or influence
which will go far towards convincing the Government of
the necessity of turning over the Indian Bureau to the
Military Department.

Gentlemen. You will please

pardon this intrusion on my part, but a sense of duty to
my Constituents prompts this action on my part.

> I am Gentlemen
> Very Respectfully
> Your Obt Servt.

> J. K. Luttrell
> Member of Congress,
> 3rd Congressional District
> California

● ● ●

FIRST DAY

FORT KLAMATH, OREGON
July 1, 1873 — 10 o'clock a. m.

The commission met pursuant to Col. Davis's Special
Field Orders No. 1, dated Fort Klamath, Oregon, June 30,
1873:

Present, (and here followed the complete roster of the
commission).

The judge-advocate then stated to the commission
that in consequence of the brief period of time he had
had since arriving at the post he had been unable to
prepare a case; and suggested an adjournment for some
days. The commission thereupon decided to adjourn until
Saturday next, the 5th instant, at 10 o'clock a.m.

Adjourned at 10 1/2 a. m.

SECOND DAY
FORT KLAMATH, July 5, 1873

The commission met at 10 a. m., pursuant to
adjournment.

Present, all of the members of the commission, the
judge-advocate, and prisoners...

The judge-advocate then read before the commission

the order convening the commission, which is interpreted to the prisoners.

The commission then proceeded to the trial of the prisoners... who being called before the commission, and having heard the order convening it read, it being interpreted to them, were severally asked if they had any objection to any member present named in the order, to which they severally replied in the negative...

... The judge-advocate then presented to the commission Dr. E. S. Belden, the official short-hand reporter, who was duly sworn to the faithful performance of his duty; which oath was duly interpreted to the prisoner.

The prisoners were then severally asked by the judge-advocate if they desired to introduce counsel; to which they severally replied in the negative; and that they had been unable to procure any.

The prisoners were then severally duly arraigned on the following charges and specifications:

Charges and specifications preferred against certain Modoc Indians commonly known and called as Captain Jack, Schonchis, Boston Charley, Black Jim, Barncho, alias One-Eyed Jim, and Sloluck, alias Cok.

CHARGE 1. "Murder, in violation of the laws of war."

SPECIFICATION 1: In this, that they, Indians, called and commonly known as Captain Jack, Schonchin, Black Jim, Boston Charley, Barncho, alias One-Eyed Jim, and Sloluck, alias Cok, members of a certain band of Indians known as the Modocs, which band, including the prisoners above named, was, at the time hereinafter alleged, engaged in open and flagrant war with the United States, under the chief command of said Captain Jack, did as representatives of said Modoc band, meet under a flag of truce and suspension of hostilities, Brig. Gen. E. R. S. Canby, U. S. A., commanding the Department of the Columbia, and certain peace commissioners on the part of the United States, namely, Eleazar

Thomas, A. B. Meacham, and L. S. Dyer, citizens of the United States, all representing the Government of the United States, for the agreed and professed purpose of discussing and arranging terms upon which hostilities existing between the United States and said band should cease, and did thereupon, in wanton violation of said flag of truce, and treacherously disregarding the obligations imposed by said truce under the laws of war, willfully, feloniously, and of malice aforethought, kill and murder said Brigadier General Canby.

"All this at or near the lava beds, so-called, situated near Tule Lake, in the State of California, on or about the 11th day of April, A.D. 1873."

SPECIFICATION 2: "In this, that they, Indians, called and commonly known as Captain Jack, Schonchis, Black Jim, Boston Charley, Barncho, alias One-Eyed Jim, and Sloluck, alias Cok, members of a certain band of Indians known as the Modocs, which band, including the prisoners above named, was at the time and place hereinafter alleged, engaged in open and flagrant war with the United States, under the chief command of said Captain Jack, did as representatives of said Modoc band, meet under a flag of truce and suspension of hostilities, Brig. Gen. E. R. S. Canby, U. S. A., commanding the Military Department of the Columbia, and certain peace commissioners on the part of the United States, namely, Eleazer Thomas, A. B. Meacham, and L. S. Dyar, citizens of the United States, all representing the Government of the Unites States, for the agreed and professed purpose of discussing and arranging terms upon which the hostililties existing between the United State and said band should cease, and did thereupon, in wanton violation of the sacred character of said flag or truce, and treacherously disregarding the obligations imposed by such truce under the laws of war, willfully, feloniously, and of their malice aforethought, kill and murder said Eleazer Thomas, one of the peace commissioners aforesaid.

"All this at or near the lava beds, so-called, situated

near Tule Lake, in the State of California, on or about the
11th day of April, A. D. 1873."

CHARGE 2. "Assault, with intent to kill, in violation
of the laws of war."

SPECIFICATION 1: "In this, that they, Indians,
called and commonly known as Captain Jack, Schonchis,
Boston Charley, Black Jim, Barncho, alias One-Eyed Jim,
and Sloluck, alias Cok, members of a certain band of
Indians known as the Modocs, which band, including the
prisoners above named, was, at the time hereinafter
alleged, engaged in open and flagrant war with the
United States, under the chief command of said Captain
Jack, did, as representatives of said Modoc band, meet,
under a flag of truce and suspension of hostilities, Brig.
Gen. E. R. S. Canby, U. S. A., commanding the Department of the Columbia, and certain peace commissioners
on the part of the United States, namely, Eleazer
Thomas, A. B. Meacham, and L. S. Dyer, citizens, all
representing the Government of the United States, for
the agreed and professed purpose of discussing and
arranging terms upon which the hostilities existing
between the United States and said band should cease;
and did thereupon, in wanton violation of the sacred
character of said flag of truce, and treacherously
disregarding the obligations imposed by such truce
under the laws of war, feloniously make an assault with
deadly weapons upon the said A. B. Meacham, then and
there feloniously, willfully, and of malice aforethought
to kill and murder, and did inflict upon the body of said
Meacham divers, severe and dangerous wounds.

"All this at or near the lava beds, so-called, situated
near Tule Lake, in the State of California, on or about the
11th day of April, A. D. 1873.

SPECIFICATION 2: "In this, that they, Indians,
called and commonly known as Captain Jack, Schonchis,
Boston Charley, Black Jim, Barncho, alias One-Eyed Jim,
and Sloluck, alias Cok, members of a certain band

Indians known as Modocs, which band, including the prisoners above named, was at the time and place hereinafter alleged, engaged in open and flagrant war with the United States under the chief command of said Captain Jack, did as representatives of said Modoc band, meet under a flag of truce and suspension of hostilities, Brig. Gen. E. R. S. Canby, U. S. A. and certain peace commissioners on the part of the United States, namely, Eleazer Thomas, A. B. Meacham, and L. S. Dyer, citizens, all representing the Government of the United States, for the agreed and professed purpose of discussing and arranging terms upon which hostilities existing between the United States and said band should cease, and did then and there, in wanton violation of said flag of truce, and treacherously disregarding the obligations imposed by such truce under the laws of war, feloniously make an assault with deadly weapons upon said Dyer, commissioner as aforesaid, with intent him, said Dyer, then and there feloniously, willfully, and of their malice afore-thought, to kill and murder.

"All of this at or near the lava beds, so-called, situated near Tule Lake, in the State of California, on or about the 11th day of April, 1873."

To which the prisoners severally pleaded as follows:
To first specification, first charge, "Not guilty."
To second specification, first charge, "Not guilty."
To first charge, "Not guilty."
To first specification, second charge, "Not guilty"
To second specification, second charge, "Not guilty."
To second charge, "Not guilty."...

● ● ●

(After the trial,...)
The commission was then closed for deliberation, and having maturely considered the evidence adduced, find the prisoner, known as Captain Jack, [reported] as follows:

Of the first specification, charge 1, "Guilty."

Of the second specification, charge 1, "Guilty."
Of charge 1, "Guilty."
Of first specification, charge 2, "Guilty."
Of second specification, charge 2, "Guilty."
Of charge 2, "Guilty."

And the commission does therefore sentence him, Captain Jack, to be hanged by the neck until he be dead, at such time and place as the proper authority shall direct; two-thirds of the members of the commission concurring therein.

And the commission do find the prisoner known as Schonchis as follows:
Of the first specification, charge 1, "Guilty."
Of the second specification, charge 1, "Guilty." Of charge 1, "Guilty."
Of first specification, charge 2, "Guilty." Of second specification, charge 2, "Guilty."
Of charge 2, "Guilty."
And the commission does therefore sentence him, Schonchis, to be hanged by the neck until he be dead, at such time and place as the proper authority shall direct; two-thirds of the members of the commission concurring therein.

And the commission do find the prisoner, Boston Charley, as follows:
Of the first specification, charge 1, "Guilty."
Of the second specification, charge 1, "Guilty."
Of charge 1, "Guilty."
Of first specification, charge 2, "Guilty."
Of second specification, charge 2, "Guilty."
Of charge 2, "Guilty."
And the commission does therefore sentence him, Boston Charley, to be hanged by the neck until he be dead, at such time and place as the proper authority shall direct; two-thirds of the members of the commission concurring therein.

And the commission do find the prisoner, Black Jim, as follows:
Of the first specification, charge 1, "Guilty."
Of the second specification, charge 1, "Guilty."
Of charge 1, "Guilty."
Of first specification, charge 2, "Guilty."
Of second specification, charge 2, "Guilty."
Of charge 2, "Guilty."
And the commission does therefore sentence him, Black Jim, to be hanged by the neck until he be dead, at such time and place as the proper authority shall direct; two-thirds of the members of the commission concurring therein.

And the commission do find the prisoner, Barncho, as follows: Of the first specification, charge 1, "Guilty." Of the second specification, charge 1, "Guilty."
Of charge 1, "Guilty."
Of first specification, charge 2, "Guilty."
Of second specification, charge 2, "Guilty."
Of charge 2, "Guilty."
And the commission does therefore sentence him, Barncho, to be hanged by the neck until he be dead, at such time and place as the proper authority shall direct; two-thirds of the members of the commission concurring therein.

And the commission do find the prisoner, Schloluck, or Cok, as follows:
Of the first specification, charge 1, "Guilty."
Of the second specification, charge 1, "Guilty."
Of charge 1, "Guilty."
Of first specification, charge 2, "Guilty."
Of second specification, charge 2, "Guilty."
Of charge 2, "Guilty."
And the commission does therefore sentence him, Schloluck, alias Cok, to be hanged by the neck until he be dead, at such time and place as the proper authority shall direct; two-thirds of the members of the commission concurring therein.

W. L. ELLIOTT,
Lieut. Col. First Cavalry,
President Mil. Com.

H. P. CURTIS,
Major, U.S.A.,
Judge-Advocate Mil. Com.

● ● ●

(Letter)

Yreka Siskiyou County Cal
July 3rd 1873

Hon C Delano
Sec Int.

Sir

herewith please find petition in matter of Modoc
Indians— It is a matter I have no interest in other than
any other citizen of our Country—

These indians are used to take care of themselves,
talk our language & understand all kinds of farm work-
They ask the privilege & name Mr Burgess as they have
full confidence in his integrity towards them— He can
use them to advantage & will pay them wages that will
support them well -

As to the other Indians, Capt Jack & others whom it
seems fated must be executed — permit me to ask an
interference to the extent of working a delay until a full
& fair investigation of the causes of the war, be had, as
they are very important witnesses

I ask this as Mr Odeneal officially & through the
Oregon papers has persistently attacked my character &
that of others including one District Judge Rosborough
and we are anxious that the whole matter be ventilated
& the truth exposed

Very Respect Your
obt Servant

E Steele

• • •

FORT KLAMATH, OREGON

July 8, 1873

COLONEL: The telegram from you stopping other trials by this commission than that of the assassins of General Canby and the peace commissioners, was received by me this morning. The trial of the slayers of Lieutenant Sherwood is not prohibited by it, but that case it is impossible to try, for the reason that of the three Indians who are suspected of committing the murder, one, Curly-headed Jack, has killed himself. Miller's Charley is not in custody, and the third cannot be known or identified.

Lieutenant Davis, on leaving for Camp Warner and Portland, handed me a list of the able-bodied Modocs in arrest here, but did not designate whom I was to try. Four of these Modocs, namely, Steamboat Frank, Hooker Jim, Bogus Charley, and Shacknasty Jim, are known as scouts. They were employed, as you know, in pursuing others of the hostile band, and, according to every testimony, did most efficient and faithful service, and did very much toward shortening the war. I decided not to arraign them for their participation in the assassination of General Canby, therefore, though all were more or less concerned in it.

I am not aware that General Davis promised them immunity; but I am assured by Captain Hasbrouck, Fourth Artillery, and others, that they proved themselves of the highest efficiency and value, so much so as to earn protection from punishment; and I learn from Mr. Riddle, the interpreter, that he, himself, translated to Hooker Jim an assurance from the lips of Colonel Green, lately commanding this post, in the following words, or nearly: "You will not be hurt — you shall not be hurt."

Additional to this their treatment by General Davis
while in his hands has been such as seemed to me to be
virtually a promise of protection from the punishment of
their crimes; for they are left wholly free, permitted to
go unguarded about the fort, and might leave the place
at any time if they saw fit. I was told by General Davis
that I might try them if I pleased, but he recommended
their employment as witnesses in the character of State's
evidence. Of the four, I believe Hooker Jim the worst by
far. Him I had intended to use, if possible, in the trial of
the Lost River murderers of citizens in 1872.

Should it be the intention of the Government to turn
over to the State authorities such prisoners as were
indicted for these murders, I believe it my duty to urge
that these four men be reserved from that fate, both
because of their services in ending the war, and of the
quasi promises which would seem to have been made
them that they should be protected. I am informed that
the indictments were found on the information of Mrs.
William Boddy, and that of those indicted several are
known to have had no part in the murders referred to,
and that Mrs. Boddy made more than one mistake in her
designation of the guilty.

I have omitted to state an additional reason which
influenced me in deciding not to arraign the four
so-called scouts. I believed that there could be no better
policy than that of teaching these savages that treachery
to their race, under such circumstances as those which
have obtained here, would meet with its sure reward. I
may have been wrong in permitting this consideration to
have weight; but, left to decide the question of their trial
by my own unaided judgement, I could do not otherwise
than act in accordance with what seemed the wisest
course.

I therefore respectfully invite attention to the claims
of these four men, all of whom testified to-day at the
trail of the slayers of General Canby and Dr. Thomas.

Very respectfully, your obedient servant,
H. P. CURTIS,

Judge Advocate Commission

Lieut. Col. J. C. KELTON,
   A.A.G., Military Division Pacific

P.S. — I should, perhaps, more properly have addressed this communication to, or through, General Davis, commanding this Department, but he is now on his march through the country toward Portland, and the necessity of haste seems to me to require a deviation from the usual course.

H. P. CURTIS,
Judge-Advocate

● ● ●

Klamath Agency, Oregon,
July 8. 1873

Hon Edw. Smith, Commissioner
   Indian Affairs

I have to report my arrival, on the 5th Inst. at this place. The Military Commission to try Modoc prisoners will probably conclude its present labors within a few days. All the witnesses have testified and Capt. Jack will conclude his "statement" tomorrow.

The ruling of the commission excludes all irrelevant evidence, not strictly touching the assassination. Wide range is allowed prisoners in making statements. Nothing new however has been brought out implicating outside parties in either the matter of assassination or of the origin of the war.

Having no authority to examine witnesses, I am not in condition to accomplish very much in the matter of obtaining reliable information touching the Rebellion of the Modocs.

I have received letter of June 21. in relation to funds, but none containing instruction or authority to investigate. I will remain here a few days after the Military

Commission closes and, unless otherwise ordered, will then visit my home in Salem, Oregon.

The public are dissatisfied with the present understanding in regard to Modocs who are taken into service of Gen. Davis, on promise of protection and pardon. These four are really very bad men. The statement of prisoners on trial confirms the assertion. You will understand, doubtless that the few men referred to are not on trial, neither are they confined or ironed but enjoy the liberty of the camp at Fort Klamath.

I have no positive information on the subject but doubt not the civil authorities will make a demand on [illegible] military for two at least of the four exempt Indians. Serious questions will probably arise as I am of the opinion that the military authorities will feel bound by the promises made to the Modocs referred to protect them from trial. I do not believe they should be allowed to escape trial and punishment unless the promises were made by the knowledge and approval of those having full authority in the premises, and even then it is unjust.

> Very Respectfully
> Your Obt. Servt.
>
> A B Meacham

• • •

(letter)
Head Qrs
Fort Klamath Oregon
July 9, 1873

1st Lieut W. H. Boyle 21' Infty
   A A A G. Dept of the Columbia "in the field"

I have the honor to report that the military Commission has this day completed all the business relative to the trial of the Modocs and therefore adjourned Sine Die.

H. C. Hasbrouck
Capt 4th Artillery, Comd'g

• • •

(letter)

Fort Klamath, Oregon
July 9, 1873

Bvt Maj. Gen. Jeff C. Davis
Commg Dpt. Columbia

General:

I have the honor to forward the record of the trial of the assassins of Gen - Canby & Dr. Thomas; Six in number- I thought it best you not having given me positive Instructions on the subject, to omit from the list of those whom I arraigned, the four men known as scouts, namely Hocker [sic] Jim, Bogus Charley, Shacknasty Jim, and Steamboat Frank. My motive for this was partly because their treatment since surrender seemed to me to be a virtual period of immunity from punishment; and partly because it appeared to me good policy to teach these savages that treachery to their tribe will meet with its sure reward.

In the case of the murder of Lieut. Sherwood, I found it impossible to discover evidence to identify its perpetrators.

The enclosed telegram will show why I have not prosecuted the investigation, which I had commenced into the question of the Lost River murders of Novr. 1872. This telegram I received day before yesterday - of course after your departure from this Post.

The Court adjourned Sine die this day.

I have the honor to be

Very respy
Yr. obedt. svt

H. P. Curtis
Maj. J. A. U. S. A.
J. A. of Commissn

• • •

JULY 29, 1873

The proceedings and findings of the military commis-
sion in the above cases of Captain Jack, Schonchis,
Boston Charley, Black Jim, Barncho, Schloluck or Cok,
Modoc Indian prisoners, are approved, and the sentences
are confirmed. In compliance with War Department
General Order Number 72, July 7, 1873, they are
respectfully transmistted to the Bureau of Military
Justice, to be laid before the President for his orders.
JEF. C. DAVIS,
Col. and Bvt. Maj.-Genl. U.S.A.
Reviewing Officer

• • •

To the Hon C. Delano
Secretary of Interior
The undersigned Citizens of Siskiyou County Cal. would
respectfully represent - that of the Modoc Indians now
held as prisoners of war there are some that no charges
are made against except open warfare against the United
States of which are Scarfaced Charley and Miller's
Charley — that there are others who for services
rendered as scouts in the capture and subjugation of the
tribe have rendered material aid to the government and
earned an exemption from rigorous punishment of which
are Bogus Charley, Shacknasty Jim, Hooka Jim and
Steamboat Frank - the so called scouts.
We would also state that all of these Indians are
useful farm hands, capable of and fully competent
intellectually to trade for and take care of themselves —
that they have expressed a desire to make their own
living and be no burden to the government — that they

be allowed to seek employment for themselves & to enter
the service of John C. Burgess, late Sheriff of Siskiyou
County Cal, who is a large farmer near Yreka.

We would therefor respectfully ask that they be
permitted to enter the service of said Burgess upon such
conditions as shall be deemed advisable - Yreka July
30th 1873 -

> Very Respectfully Yours
> E Steele
> Wm H Morgan Sheriff,
> John A Fairchild
> H Wallace Atwell
> alias Bill Dadd,
> > the Scribe

• • •

Yreka July 30th 1873

Hon C Delano,   Secty Interior

Sir,
    You will pardon me in troubling you with a request
to defer action on the finding of the commission
appointed to try Cap Jack and other Moadoc prisoners,
untill a full and fair investigation of the causes leading
to that sad affair for which they were tried can be had.
We ask that a Commissioner be appointed, with power to
send for and compell the attendance of witnesses, who
otherwise could keep very clear of an investigating
committee.
    We know that those prisoners who were tried without
counsel, and before their counsel was aware that the day
of the trial had been named. We know that the general
belief is the Interpreter employed is unworthy of
credence. We know he is illiterate, can neither read or
write, can not translate the idioms of our tongue, can not
even understand good english. We know the squaw with
whom he cohabits has shielded her relatives in her

Interpreting, at the expense of others,

We know that gross wrongs have been committed by
whites on these Indians and will show them if permitted
to do so We can and will show much in mitigation of the
offences committed by these Moadocs, will show this war
was brought about by designing men for selfish purposes, And we will show gross mismanagement and treachery on the part of those whose positions should have
been a guarantee of fair dealing.

For these reasons and that the fair fame of some of
the best citizens of this county may be cleared, and the
guilty exposed, we pray you to appoint an Impartial
Commission of three, men who do not live on this coast,
and let us sift this matter to the bottom. For the credit of
the government and the cause of humanity it should not
rest here. I have been in the campaign from the first,
been in nearly all the battles, acting as war corespondent
for the Sacramento Record, and toward the last for the N
Y Herald. I was with the Peace Commission all the time,
was in the cave on two embassies with Mr Steel,

Therefore I claim I have a right to know whereof I
speak. Having been on the coast for twenty two years,
having a good knowledge of Indians and their ways, I
can not, in common with thousands, avoid the feeling
that a great wrong has been committed and should be
investigated for the honor of our Government which is
supposed to protect the weak My address is Sacramento
city,

> I have the honor to remain
> Your Obt Servt
>
> H Wallace Atwell

"Bill Dadd the Scribe"

• • •

EXECUTIVE OFFICE, August 22, 1873

The foregoing sentences in the cases of Captain Jack,

Schonchis, Black Jim, Boston Charley, Barncho alias
One-Eyed Jim, and Sloluck alias Cok, Modoc Indian
prisoners, are hereby approved; and it is ordered that the
sentences in said cases be carried into execution by the
proper military authority, under the orders of the
Secretary of War, on the third day of October, eighteen
hundred and seventy three.

U. S. GRANT,
President

• • •

WAR DEPARTMENT,
Washington, August 23, 1873

The foregoing record of the proceedings in the trial by
military commission of Captain Jack, Schonchis, Black
Jim, Boston Charley, Barncho alias One-Eyed Jim, and
Sloluck alias Cok, Modoc Indian prisoners, having been
transmitted to the President and laid before him for his
orders thereon; and the President having in the foregoing orders approved of the sentences and directed that
they be executed under the orders of the Secretary of
War, the sentences will be duly executed under the
direction of the general commanding the Department of
Columbia, at Fort Klamath, Oregon, on Friday, October 3,
1873.

WILLIAM W. BELKNAP,
Secretary of War.

By order of the Secretary of War,
E. D. TOWNSEND, Adjutant General.

• • •

[Extract from a private letter of Major Curtis, judge-
advocate of the Modoc military commission, to an officer in
the Judge-Advocate- General's office, Washington.]
"I would like to have said a word in favor of lenity

toward Barncho and Sloluck. The others were all
involved deeply in the plot to murder, consulted about it
with each other, and acted as ringleaders, I have no
doubt. B. and S., however, I regard as common soldiers,
who obeyed orders in being present, or rather within
hail, and whom it will be an unnecessary outlay of
national vengeance to put to death. They both took no
visible interest in the trial, and I doubt if they
understood it. Sloluck sat with his hands over his face
and much of the time on the floor, apparently asleep. He
is quite a boy, at least in looks. Barncho was little better.
Neither of them, I believe,· could have taken any
prominent part in the war, or anything. One of them
knocked down Mrs. Riddle and seized her horse, but did
her no injury."

CHAPTER 7

PAGAN PRELIMINARIES

(Letter)

Head Qrs Fort Klamath, Oregon
August 7, 1873

Capt. H. C. Hasbrouck
    4' Arty Officer of the Day
Sir,
    I am directed to request you to examine the Modoc
Prisoners in confinement at this Post, with a view of
issuing them such articles of clothing from the supply of
the Troops as may be actually necessary to prevent
unusual suffering.
    The Indian prisoners will be directed to wash and
clean such articles of clothing now in their possession as
can be made of any service, the remainder will be buried
after it has been replaced by new.
    Damaged clothing will be issued by the A A Q M if on
hand

Very Respectfully,
Geo W. Kingsbury
2nd Lt. 12' Inftry
Post Adjutant

(Telegram)

Head Qrs. Fort Klamath, Ogn
Aug. 8, 1873

The Asst Adjt Gen.
    Dept Columbia.
In order to prevent disease and sickness from filth and

vermin, authority to issue requisite clothing to Indian Prisoner of War in confinement at Fort Klamath is requisite.

> (Frank Wheaton)
> Lt Col 21' Inftry
> Comd'g Post.

• • •

(Dispatch)

— THE MODOCS —
Closing Scenes of the Tragedy
A "Chronicle" Correspondent at Fort Klamath
SORROWFUL SCENES IN CAMP

Captain Jack and His Five Companions to be Hanged To-Day — [No, tomorrow, October 3rd] The Doomed Chieftain and His Family Preparation for the Execution of the Doomed Indians A MAMMOTH GALLOWS — The Six Savages to Drop at One Signal All of the Indian Tribes — Collected to Witness the Execution Citizens of Jacksonville and Ashland Flocking to the Scene. (BY TELEGRAPH FROM THE CHRONICLE'S SPECIAL REPORTER)

YREKA, Cal., October 2d

A courier from the CHRONICLE'S special correspondent at Fort Klamath, 122 miles from this point, has just arrived with the following dispatches:

> FORT KLAMATH,
> Jackson County,
> Oregon, September 30th.

The preparations for the execution of Captain Jack, Schonchin, Boston Charley, Black Jim, Sloluck and Barncho are almost complete. Today the post carpenter began the construction of

THE GALLOWS

The condemned savages are to be hanged together.
They will all drop at one signal. The beam is to be thirty
feet in length. Promptly at 10 o'clock on Friday morning
the Modoc will be led out to their death. Captain George B.
Hoge, of Company G, Twelfth Infantry, has been detailed
as officer of the day. On him, on that occasion, will
devolve the trying duty of strangling the six warriors.
Captain Hoge, during the war of the rebellion, was
Colonel of the One Hundred and Thirteenth Illinois
Volunteers, and subsequently served as Provost Marshal
General of East Tennessee. The scaffold is erected on the
south side of the Fort, in an open field, two hundred
yards distant from the stockade, where are confined the
remainder of the captive tribe, numbering one hundred
and sixty-two, all told. The execution is to be as public as
possible, the object being to

ASSEMBLE ALL THE INDIANS

So that they may be forever terrified by the spectacle.
The Klamaths, whose reservation (agency) is situated
four miles south of this station, are all coming to witness
the tragedy. It is also understood that the scaffold, when
finished, will be at such an elevation that the captive
Modocs confined in the stockade can, by peeping through
the apertures, view the execution.

OREGONIANS COMING

The mountain roads from Jacksonville and Ashland to
this place are reported as filled with Oregonians, hurry-
ing, in all descriptions of vehicles, to be in at the death.
Many of the settlers in the Rogue River Valley are on
their way here. The "reliable gentleman" from Ashland
tells me that one school in that town has been given a
week's holiday, so as to enable the preceptor and pupils to
come here and gloat over the ghastly scene. But few from
Yreka will be on hand, as the Siskiyou County Fair begins
this week. The military forces at this station consists of
Troop B, First Cavalry; Companies E and G, Twelfth
Infantry; Companies F and D, Twenty-first Infantry, and
Hasbrouck's Light Battery B, Fourth Artillery; in all,

about 300 men. The troops will form a hollow square, with the scaffold in the center, the spectators having ample room outside the military line to witness the execution.

Up to this time the condemned Indians have betrayed no emotion over their impending fate. Captain Jack is showing evidence of weakness. He eats little, and complains of pain in his hip and his left arm, which was broken some years ago by a fall from his horse when hunting , and Doctor Cabaniss says that the chieftain is afflicted with neuralgia in the hip.

AN AFFECTING INCIDENT

Occurred here yesterday. Captain Jack was allowed to visit his wives in the stockade. Scarfaced Charley carried a box over to him, and Jack's wife, Lizzie, a shawl, which she spread over the box. Captain Jack then seated himself. At this time his youngest child, a little girl about four years of age, ran toward her father, rending the air with frantic screams. Captain Jack extended both his arms to receive his infant daughter, and at the same time turned his head aside. For several minutes he maintained this position unchanged, embracing the child and with averted head; yet his countenance gave no indication of the great emotion which must have stirred his innermost soul.

All the members of the tribe looked on, maintaining a most stoical silence. A few moments later an old Indian crept up with a lighted pipe, which he gently and almost reverently placed in the chieftain's mouth. Neither of his wives spoke one word to him; in fact, from the time he entered until he was conducted back to his cell not one word passed between the condemned chieftain and his imprisoned followers.

All the asperities created in the tribe by the quarrel between the Hot Creek band and the Lost River band have melted away before the appalling dread which attends the coming tragedy. Some of the squaws are already blackening their faces as a symbol of grief. The Modocs are united in sympathy and friendship once more.

The impending fate of their chief and five of his best warriors has healed all the animosities engendered by this memorable Indian campaign.

THE GUARD-HOUSE,

A reformatory institution connected with all well-regulated military encampments, is to be the home of the six doomed Modocs up to the hour of their death. This is a small whitewashed frame building, situated immediately to the right of the stockade. The guard-house affords accommodations for the sentinels on the off watches; or in other words, is the rendezvous of the camp guard. It is one story in height, with a sloping roof. A covered stoop, approached by three steps, distinguishes the front. The windows are barred with iron. The interior is by no means inviting.

On the right hand, upon entering, are three doors, each leading to the cells where lie huddled together the subjugated savages. The rear apartment is occupied by thirty six soldiers, in durance for various offenses against good order and military discipline. To-day your correspondent visited this place. Lieutenant Anderson, the officer of the day, kindly escorted him to the premises. The sergeant of the guard unlocked the grim padlock which held fast the first door.

A STRANGE SCENE

Challenged the eye and a stranger odor attacked the nose. So closely packed were the Indians that there was hardly room to enter without treading on them. The cell was very small, its dimensions being about eight feet square. Seven Modocs sat on three sides of the wall facing the door. Though the day was sultry and the heat oppressive, all of these copper-colored children of the forest were buried in their blankets. Four of the seven had but a few days to live.

Brightly polished steel manacles, riveted on the feet of all, glistened in the sunlight streaming through the barred windows, and rattled and clinked as the savages drew their legs up until their knees nearly touched their

chins. The seven prisoners were Boston Charley, Black
Jim, Long Jim, Schonchin Pete, Sloluck, Barncho, Ike,
and the Curly-headed Doctor's brother (son). Of these,
Boston Charley, Black Jim, Barncho, and Sloluck were
doomed. The first two named were manacled together, as
were also the latter two. With their great brown eyes, the
captives one and all, gazed on their visitors. The look was
rather scrutinizing than searching.

THEIR APPEARANCE

They were all healthy looking Indians, and young in
years; in form and features they differed but little -
massive chests, and broad, square set shoulders, large
heads abundantly covered with black, straight hair,
parted in the middle and sloping down below the ears to
the chin; complexions varying from a sickly yellow to a
deep burnished olive; noses large and prominent; fore-
heads low; eyes deep set, large and lustrous; mouths large
and firmly set, now and then revealing a row of
glistening white teeth; lips almost colorless and destitute
of expression, and cheeks chubby and flabby. This may
answer for a general description of the Modoc. He is not
sullen, for at times his features light up with a smile that
is neither senile nor bland, and his hand-shake is cordial,
almost fraternal. Of the seven Indians who sat cooped up
in this contracted space, Boston Charley seemed to feel
his imprisonment the most.

Dr. Cabaniss, one of the post surgeons, who was a
conspicuous figure in the campaign, was among the
visitors. As the Doctor turned to leave, Boston Charley
clutched him nervously by the arm, exclaiming: "Want to
see little while; come soon; want talk." The Doctor
promised to look in upon him again, whereupon Charley
gloomily slumped into his sitting posture. The adjoining
cell, narrower, smaller and darker, was occupied by

CAPTAIN JACK AND SCHONCHIN

When the door was swung in on its hinges these two
warrior chiefs were observed lying on the floor. Jack was
asleep. A gray blanket covered him from head to foot. He

was lying furthest from the entrance, with his feet toward the door. Schonchin was lying on his right side, his head elevated and resting on his elbow. Both wore fetters, but they were not manacled together. Jack was aroused by the officer of the day, who told the chief that some gentlemen from a long way off had called to see him. The doomed chieftain slowly arose, came forward and extended his right hand to each of the visitors. His big hand was clammy, but warm. His grasp, though weak, was cordial. He said nothing, but with his keen piercing eyes looked full into the faces of his visitors.

Jack has all the physical characteristics of his tribe already noted. His forehead is higher than the others. He is about five feet eight inches in height, and of dark complexion. His mouth is rather repulsive; his hair parted in the middle. He wore a gray shirt and blue army trowsers. Schonchin made no sign. He is taller and evidently older than Jack. The hard lines in his face gave him a repugnant look. His eyes are dull and heavy. He neither shook hands nor moved a muscle of his face during the interview.

The third cell was occupied by the Curly-headed Doctor, Dave, and One-Eyed Mose. The two latter were chained together.

THE CURLY-HEADED DOCTOR

Is a stalwart savage, about six feet high, and of marked muscular development. He wore a clean white flannel shirt. His complexion is very fair, almost approaching the half-breed. He was the most cheerful Indian met. A fat smile spread over his face, and he appeared to really enjoy the intrusion, shaking hands with much enthusiasm.

● ● ●

— ONE DAY LATER —

JACKSONVILLE (Oregon), October 2d

A courier from your correspondent at Fort Klamath, 80 miles from this place, has just arrived with the annexed report:

FORT KLAMATH, October 1st.
MODOCS KILLED IN THE LAVA BEDS

Scarfaced Charley made a statement to General Wheaton to-day which shows that the Modoc losses in the late war were much greater than at first reported or supposed. He gave the names of twenty who were killed and six who were wounded. This includes four squaws, one girl twelve years of age, one pappoose, the four Modoc warriors who were murdered while being escorted under guard to this station, and Curly-haired Jack, who committed suicide.

WHAT IS TO BE DONE WITH THE TRIBE
From a reliable source it is ascertained that the United States Government will not turn over to the Oregon authorities the Indians indicted for murder of the settlers on Lost river. An order has been received here, directing the transfer of the entire tribe, after the execution of Captain Jack and his five accomplices in the Canby Massacre, to Fort D. A. Russell, in Wyoming Territory.

Battery B of the Fourth United States Artillery, under command of Captain Hasbrouck, is detailed to escort the band to its new reservation. There will be in the extradited band 39 bucks, 55 squaws and 62 children - 156 in all. They will be marched from here to Redding, and thence taken on the cars to Sacramento and thence to Wyoming.

TESTING THE GALLOWS
Today the gallows on which the condemned Indians are to die was tested by the suspension of sand-bags corresponding to their weight, from the beam. It is an enormous structure.

USELESS CRUELTY

Lieutenant Kingsbury, the Post Adjutant, is to read at the scaffold the proceedings and findings of the Military Commission and the orders of the President, the Secretary of War, and General Schofield, in relation to the execution of the sentence.

Riddle has been sent for to interpret the reading to the condemned.

If this portion of the programme is carried out, the doomed savages must stand on the scaffold with the ropes around their necks for more than an hour before the drop falls.

CAPTAIN JACK

Is still greatly distressed over his sore hip, and begins to look very haggard.

The Doctors attribute his illness to acute mental anxiety. He eats but little food. Boston Charley, the murderer of Dr. Thomas, is the most despondent of the other five. He said to-day that he did not want to die, and that he wanted to see Gen. Davis. It is generally believed in camp that Captain Jack will utterly break down on the scaffold, while not a few contend that he will exhibit all the stoic fortitude of his race.

● ● ●

CHAPTER 8

THE LAST MISERABLE MILE

THE DEAD MODOCS
Further Details of the Execution
Captain Jack Weakens on the Threshold of the Spirit
Land
Boston Charley Chews Tobacco and Dies Game
A Terrible Lesson for the Indians

At 1 o'clock this morning, when Lieut. Taylor, the officer of the day, made his rounds, all was quiet in the guard-house. Jack and Schonchin were sound asleep; the other two were also in a deep slumber. Lieutenant Taylor, through Scarfaced Charley, told Barncho and Sloluck that their sentence was commuted to imprisonment for life at Alcatraz Island. They did not at first understand the order, Barncho saying that Wheaton ordered him yesterday to be hanged, and he expected to die. Sloluck afterward said that his heart was sick, but he was glad to live.

The scaffold upon which the Modocs were executed was completed yesterday and all preparations perfected before sunset. To-day it only remained to execute and in accordance with the President's order and the orders of the Secretary of war and the Department Commander: Captain Jack, Schonchin, Black Jim, and Boston Charley, paid the highest penalty of the law — "To be hanged by the neck until dead, at such time and place as the proper authority shall direct, two-thirds of the members of the Commission concurring therein".

The morning was beautiful and clear. A line of troops was formed on the Fort parade at 9 o'clock a.m. precisely under the direction of the Post Adjutant, Lieut. Kingsbury, in the following order: Light Battery "B", 4th Artillery,

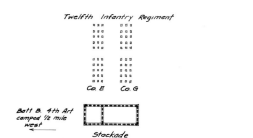

Twelfth Infantry Regiment

Co. E   Co. G

Batt B. 4th Art
camped ½ mile
west

Stockade

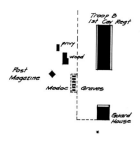

Troop B
1st Cav Regt

privy

wood

Post
Magazine

Modoc   Graves

Guard
House

ENLARGEMENT

100   o ft   100   200

N

22 | 23
27 | 26

Gallows

Map III

CURLY - HEADED DOCTOR.

I certify that L. HELLER has this day taken the Photographs of the above
Modoc Indian, prisoner under my charge.
Capt. C. B. THROCKMORTON, 4th U. S. Artillery, Officer of the Day.
I am cognizant of the above fact.   GEN. JEFF. C. DAVIS, U. S. A.

Photo no. 140. Curly-Headed Doctor, Modoc Indian, and one of the tribal
shamans. Landrum Collection.

JACK'S FAMILY—Lizzy (young wife), Mary (his sister), Old Wife & Daughter

I certify that L. HELLER has this day taken the Photographs of the above
Modoc Indians, prisoners under my charge.
Capt. C. B. THROCKMORTON, 4th U. S. Artillery, Officer of the Day.
I am cognizant of the above fact.   GEN. JEFF. C. DAVIS, U. S. A.

Published by WATKINS, Yosemite Art Gallery, 22 & 26 Montgomery St., opp. Lick House

Photo no. 145. Captain Jack's family. Lizzie, young wife; Princess Mary, sister; Rebecca, old wife; in front, Rose, Capt. Jack's and Rebecca's daughter. Landrum Collection.

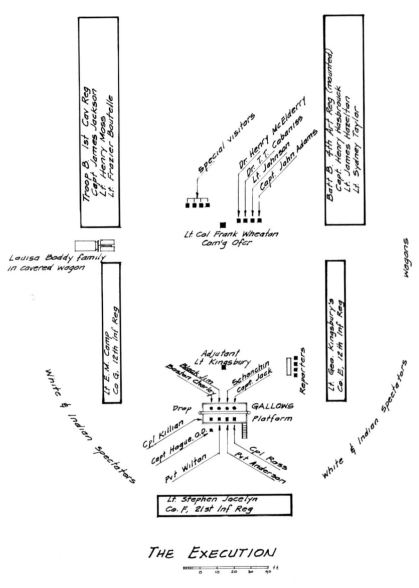

Troop B 1st Cav Reg
Capt James Jackson
Lt. Henry Moss
Lt. Frazier Boutelle

Special visitors

Dr. Henry McElderry
Dr. T. T. Cabaniss
Lt. Johnson
Capt. John Adams

Batt B. 4th Art Reg (mounted)
Capt. Henry Hasbrouck
Lt. James Hazelton
Lt. Sydney Taylor

Lt. Col Frank Wheaton
Com'g Ofcr

Louisa Boddy family
in covered wagon

Lt. E. M. Camp
Co. G. 12th Inf Reg

wagons

White & Indian Spectators

Adjutant
Lt Kingsbury

Black Jim
Boston Charley

Schonchin
Capt. Jack

Reporters

Lt. Geo. Kingsbury's
Co. E. 12th Inf Reg

Drop

GALLOWS
Platform

Cpl Killian

Capt Hogue. O.D.

Pvt Wilton

Cpl Ross

Pvt Anderson

white & Indian Spectators

Lt. Stephen Jocelyn
Co. F, 21st Inf Reg

THE EXECUTION

0   10   20   30   40   ft

Map IV

Photo no. 150. Lieut. Sydney W. Taylor, Battery B, 4th Artillery. Courtesy Mrs. Edmund Gruber. Landrum Collection.

Photo no. 160. Bvt. Maj. Gen. Frank Wheaton, Lieut. Col. 21st Infantry. Commanding officer, District of Lakes, and commander of the Modoc Expedition through the First Stronghold battle. Landrum Collection.

Photo no. 165. Capt. James Jackson, Troop B, 1st Cavalry. Fought in all Modoc war battles except one. Fisher Collection.

Photo no. 170. Lieut. Stephen P. Jocelyn, Company D, 21st Infantry.
Arrived at Fort Klamath in fall of 1873 from Camp Warner. Commanded
Company F at the execution. Landrum Collection.

Photo no. 175. Doctor Thomas T. Cabaniss, contract surgeon. Ministered to the needs of the Modoc Indian prisoners during the trial and execution period. Landrum Collection.

Photo no. 180. Doctor Henry J. McElderry, Asst. Surgeon. Head of medical department at Fort Klamath during the trial and execution of the Modoc Indian prisoners. Landrum Collection.

Photo no. 185. Fort Klamath. The six-place gallows. Photo from the original Parke watercolor. Landrum Collection.

Photo no. 195. Harold Ashley and Landrum locating the flagpole remains. Stake (center) sits atop the old, broken, flagpole butt. Ashley photo. 1962.

Photo no. 200. Fort Klamath. Looking east at the Modoc Indian graves. Cavalry barracks to the left, guard house to the right, and "officers' row" in the distance. Fisher Collection.

Photo no. 205. Fort Klamath. The Modoc Indian graves. 1939 photo. Devere Helfrich photo. Landrum Collection.

Photo no. 210. Fort Klamath. The four Modoc Indian graves. 1988 photo. Landrum Collection.

Photo no. 215. Fort Klamath. The present museum building copied after the original guardhouse. Landrum Collection.

Capt. Hasbrouck on the right, Company "E", 12th Infantry, Lieut. Kingsbury; Company "F", 21st Infantry, Lieut. Jocelyn; Company "G", 12th Infantry, Captain Hoge and Troop "B", 1st Cavalry, Capt. Jackson. Light battery "B", 4th Artillery, and Troop "B", 1st Cavalry were mounted, which arrangement brought the foot troops in the center of the Battalion.

At 9:15 o'clock a.m. the line wheeled into column and moved past the Guard house. The center of the column arriving at which it was halted and the right wing advanced sufficiently to admit the wagon containing the condemned Modocs.

The procession moved to the gallows with the drums muffled and the field music playing the Dead March. All three companies of infantry marched with arms on the right shoulder, and the cavalry and artillery with sabres drawn. A great cloud of dust heralded the approach of the column. Boston Charley and Black Jim sat in the front of the wagon, and Captain Jack and Schonchin in the rear. Captain Jack kept his blanket drawn up nearly to his ears. Boston Charley leaned forward and intently surveyed the gallows. The gallows was located in an open field, to the south of the stockade, with a low undergrowth of brush to the east about forty feet.

Arriving at the scaffold the line was formed on the three sides of a square leaving the front open, and in the following order: Light Battery "B", 4th Artillery and Company "E", 12th Infantry on the right of the scaffold facing West, Company "F", 21st Infantry in rear of the scaffold facing North, Company "G", 12th Infantry and Troop "B", 1st Cavalry on the left facing East.

Headquarters officers were posted as follows: The Adjutant, Lieut. Kingsbury, immediately in front of the scaffold and facing it from about twenty feet distant. The Commanding Officer, Gen. Wheaton, in rear of the Adjutant and one hundred feet from the scaffold. On the left of the Commanding Officer and one pace retired were Surgeon McElderry, Doctor Cabaniss, Lieutenant Johnson, and Captain Adams. The Post Quartermaster, Colonel Hoge, stood with his arms folded and on the left behind

the place on the scaffold which would soon be occupied by
Boston Charley. Corporal Thomas Ross, Private Eugene
Anderson, and Private Robert Wilton, all Company "G"
Twelfth Infantry and Corporal John Killian, Battery "B"
Fourth Artillery were the four enlisted men charged with
the execution and stood to the right of Colonel Hoge.

On the right of the Commanding Officer and a few
paces retired was assigned a position for a few specially
favored spectators, while on line with the Adjutant and
to his left was a table with writing materials occupied by
the Reporters. On rear of the line were mounted patrols to
keep the curious at a proper distance from the troops.

Nearly three hundred Klamath Indians, squaws and
bucks, arrived at the fort at daylight, mounted on ponies.
They dismounted and took a position behind the troops.
Mrs. Boddy and her family occupied seats in a covered
wagon behind the cavalry. Several other wagons, filled
with Oregonians, were corralled in the shade of some
small pines to the right and front of the scaffold. There
were at least two thousand people including a large
number of Indians present.

Boston Charley and Black Jim ascended the scaffold
first. Boston Charley took a quid of tobacco as the stepped
out of the wagon, and another as he walked up the
scaffold stairway. He was very indifferent, looking
around at the soldiers and spitting vigorously.

CAPTAIN JACK WAS VERY WEAK

And had to be helped into the wagon at the
guard-house and assisted to his position by Corporal Ross.
Boston wore Lieutenant Cranston's cap, and Black Jim a
brown-felt slouch hat. Captain Jack and Schonchin were
uncovered. Black Jim wore a full-dress soldier's coat and
blue pants; Schonchin, an army blouse and blue trowsers.
Captain Jack wore a striped cotton shirt, which was open
at the breast, revealing a red-flanned shirt. He wore
trowsers of dark-mixed materials.

The Indians sat down on the scaffold, and were first
pinioned, under direction of Colonel Hoge, by the four
enlisted men. At five minutes to 10, (Oliver) Applegate

and Dave Hill mounted the gallows and explained to them that the orders that were about to be read were in relation to their sentence and execution. This occupied about five minutes. Schonchin, as Dave Hill descended the steps, turned round and spoke a few words to him.

Four or five dogs belonging to the garrison basked in the shadow of the gallows, which was thrown forward — the bright sun being behind the condemned. Six coffins were stored under the gallows.

Adjutant Kingsbury called the battalion to attention and read, 1st; the order promulgating the proceedings of the military commission which tried the Modocs, with the orders of the President and the Secretary of War, therein. Then an order from the department commander, directing that the execution take place at Fort Klamath, Oregon, on the 3d day of October, 1873, between the hours of 10 o'clock A.M. and 2 o'clock P.M., in accordance with the President's order.

Next, the adjutant published a post order relating to the movement of troops on this occasion and detailing all necessary arrangements for the execution, and finally, published the executive order of the President, commuting the sentences of Barncho and Sloluck to imprisonment for life, and designating Alcatraz Island, Harbor of San Francisco, as their place of confinement. While this last order was being read, the prisoners, Barncho and Sloluck were marched to the front of the scaffold and stationed directly in front of the adjutant, while the other four were sitting in their places on the scaffold.

During the reading of the orders the condemned looked around at the troops occasionally, but mainly directed their attention to the reading of the orders. They remained from the time they were pinioned until the drop fell.

Chaplain Father Charles E. Huquemborg stepped forward and read the Episcopal service for the condemned prisoners. A gentle breeze swept across the field. After the Chaplain had concluded, Colonel Hoge, who had stepped down from the gallows, approached a bucket of water, lowered a dipper and took a drink. He ascended the

gallows stairway, and directed a non-commissioned officer to carry some water to the condemned. Black Jim and
Boston each swallowed a mouthful of water. Jack and
Schonchin refused to drink. The nooses were then
adjusted.

THE BLACK CAP

Was first drawn over Jack, then another placed on
Schonchin, and another on Boston, Black Jim seeing the
sunlight last. The caps consisted of black-canvas condemned army haversacks. Three minutes of terrible
suspense followed. The condemned were then compelled
to stand up. Colonel Hoge took out a white handkerchief
and dropped it. At 10:15 o'clock, precisely, Corporal Ross
raised his hatchet, and, with a flourish, it severed the
rope and

THE DROP FELL

With a report as though one plank had fallen upon
another. The four condemned fell heavily. At the same
moment the clear voice of Captain Hasbrouck broke the
awful stillness with the command, "In parade — rest!"
Everything connected with the execution was in most
perfect order and was performed in strict military
precision. The drop was perfect and fearfully effective.
The four bodies swung round several times, and then
spun round the other way. Captain Jack and Black Jim
never moved a muscle and died without a struggle.
Schonchin and Boston Charley died hard.

The bodies were allowed to hang for thirty minutes
when they were cut down, put in their coffins and buried,
as I have before stated, in close proximity to the post
guard house where the sentinel, in death as well as life,
will watch over them and take good care that they are not
disturbed.

Again it is night, and the eventful and exciting scenes
of the day just past, contrast strangely with the quiet
moonlight evening. Just over yonder and under the
starry canopy of heaven stands an ominous structure,
with its long bare arms stretching out in the moonlight,

with trap, pillars and yards silent in death.

"Man's inhumanity to man makes countless thousands mourn." In yonder stockade to-night and in full view of the gallows, there is deep, heartfelt sorrow, and throughout the camp an undefined feeling of sympathy unsought and unexpressed, silent although potent and sincere, is too perceptible to pass unnoticed. Four immortal souls have left their earthly tenement and winged their flight to an unknown sphere, while their bodies are quietly resting side by side, buried within a few yards of the Post Guard house. Yet the measured tread of the soldier as he walks his rounds at midnight will not disturb their slumber. The inanimate bodies of the Modoc Chief and his warriors are destined to fulfil the laws of nature, "Earth to earth, dust to dust, ashes to ashes."

The majesty of the laws have been vindicated and reparation made for the sins committed as far as man is able, and although others of the Modoc tribe richly deserve death for the many cold-blooded murders they have committed, yet the example already set will be, by those surviving, long remembered.

• • •

AN EPILOGUE

The first attempt at preservation of the Fort Klamath site signalling a start at partial restoration and improvement began in 1962, a year prior to the celebration of the 100th anniversary of the Fort's founding. Proposed objectives were to determine the location of the 125 foot flagpole, preserve the graves (which had never been lost), and locate the old foundation stones of the guard house. Planned restoration included raising a replacement flagpole, building a suitable building for the guardhouse, and placing new headboards on the Modoc graves.

Fort Klamath Military Reservation and Fort Klamath Hay Reservation were surveyed and the lines marked on the ground by Captain Franklin B. Sprague before the 1872 General Land Office surveys had reached Wood River valley. Sprague tied his lines to the flagpole as the starting monument.

Fortunately for us in following years, Deputy Surveyor W. A. Owen, in running the subdivisions of Township 33 south, Range 7 "A" (now called 7 1/2) east, Willamette meridian and baseline, recorded a bearing to the flagpole. One of the section corners set by Owen in that 1872 project lies about a quarter mile from the flagpole.

From its debouchment in Upper Klamath Lake to a point one mile north of the "bridge at Fort Klamath", Wood River's left (east) bank had been defined in the Klamath Lake Indian Treaty of October 14, 1864, as a part of the western boundary of the Klamath Indian Reservation. That portion of the Fort Klamath Military Reservation on which improvements were erected lay east of the river and on the Indian reservation.

The late Harold Ashley and the writer assembled the notes from the Sprague survey, a portion of the notes of George Mercer's 1871 survey of the Klamath Indian

Reservation's riverbank boundary, and the pertinent portion of Owen's General Land Office survey. A particular fence post was pointed out by the local landowner as having been set for the section corner, that is, to perpetuate Owen's original section corner.

Using the Mercer (1871) riverbank meanders with the Owen (1872) survey, a useable course and distance could be computed from the section corner (fence post) to the flagpole. This was done, and the line was run. When the calculated distance had been marked off, Ashley, at head chain, shouted, "O.K., wise guy, where's the flagpole?"

Usually that type of question went unanswered but this answer was simple. "Turn around and look," was the reply.

Ashley was about six or seven feet from the center of a low mound, so close he actually was on the perimeter of the mound. The mound was so subtle that he couldn't see that he was on the edge of it, but coming back to the rear of the chain, he could easily see the slight raise. The "mound" was about fifteen feet in diameter and its highest elevation was only about six inches higher than the general surface of the meadow. In the center of the mound was a pronounced depression about two feet in diameter and dipping four to six inches.

Mr. William Zumbrun, the owner of the property, had warned Ashley and the writer that he would not permit digging in the field. This was a very understandable instruction as the field had been a grass prairie in 1863 when the fort was established and in the ensuing 99 years it had never been plowed. And today (1988 — 125 years later) that same fact remains true. We were looking at the same grass as did the troops.

Nevertheless, the writer was dispatched to find Mr. Zumbrun and borrow a shovel. Zumbrun came along and the three of us watched carefully. The first thrust of the spade hit wood. Enough more chunks of sod were peeled back to reveal the butt of a log about 18" diameter broken off just under the meadow turf. The flagpole was found. All of the sod was replaced and the meadow remainded unsullied.

Locating the flagpole was the first priorty for any

restoration as everything built or located in the period from 1863 to 1872 had been referenced to the flagpole as the initial monument, the key to relocating the many features of Fort Klamath, including the square-stone monuments set at each corner of the Military and Hay reservations.

Klamath County purchased about eight acres of land from the Zumbrun family and dedicated the site as a Klamath County park in August, 1973. The parcel so dedicated includes the sites of the former flagpole, guardhouse, Modoc graves, gazebo, and two barracks — one cavalry and the other an obsolete cavalry quarters.

By far the most important feature to be preserved was the group of Modoc graves. To the Klamath and Modoc Indians still residing in the Klamath country, this minute cemetery is hallowed ground, and Captain Jack is a martyr. The first photograph of the headboards of the graves was taken shortly after the new cavalry barracks was built (no one seems to have identified that date other than maybe 1874). The anonymous enterprising photographer conveniently tore off the middle board of a whitewashed fence in order to photograph the headboards. At another date Lt. John G. Parke sketched a watercolor of the scene: Headboards implanted on the raised grave mounds; easterly board fence; guard house; cavalry barracks; officers' row in the distance, and the bluff overlooking the east side of Wood River Valley.

Now just why has so much attention been paid to the Modoc graves?

Very shortly after the corpses of the four Modoc Indians had been cut down from the monstrous gallows, a prowling reporter, H. S. Shaw, was passing by a tent pitched quite near both the stockade enclosure, the guardhouse, and the graves. Inside the tent was a table covered with an "India-rubber" sheet, and resting on the sheet was a body. Surgeon Henry J. McElderry was working over the body.

QUESTION: Was the doctor treating the bodies with a solution of carbolic acid as was sometimes the custom in military embalming, or was the doctor removing the head from each Indian torso? The latter seems to have been the case. Why?

ANSWER: Quoting from "REMINISCENCES of GEORGE MARTIN KOBER, M.D., LL.D., Volume I... ...Emeritus Dean and Professor of Hygiene of the School of Medicine and Member of the Board of Regents, Georgetown University, Washington, D.C.:

"George Alexander Otis was born in Boston, Mass., Nov.12, 1830. He graduated with the degree of A.B. and A.M. from Princeton College; entered the Medical Department of the University of Pennsylvania, and received his degree of M.D. from that institution in 1850. He then visited Europe, prosecuted his studies in London and Paris, and returned to this country and established himself at Springfield, Mass... ...appointed Surgeon, U.S. Volunteers, Aug. 30, 1854. Near the close of the war he entered the Medical Corps, U.S. Army as Assistant Surgeon... ...Assigned to duty in the Office of the Surgeon General July 22, 1864, he became "Curator of the Army Medical Museum," [emphasis supplied] and was in charge of the Division of Surgical Records until his death.

"Surgeon Otis, with his personal observations of the surgical collections abroad, brought indefatigable industry and untiring energy to the development of the surgical and anatomical collections of the Army Medical Museum, which he made the most valuable of their kind in the world...

Quoting further, "I (Kober) was ordered to report for duty to Dr. Joseph J. Woodward, in charge of the Record and Pension Division, located in the Ford Theatre, on Tenth Street between E and F streets, Northwest, the scene of President Lincoln's assassination. The building housed the Army Medical Museum, the Library of the Surgeon General, and all the important records of the Army Hospitals...

Quoting still further, "Dr. Henry C. Yarrow in his reminiscences of Dr. Otis on page 73, Volume LX, of the 'MILITARY SURGEON' emphasizes the fact that one of Otis' favorite studies in later life was the examination of the cranium. He, like Professor Virchow, evidently was especially interested in the crania of North American Indians, of which the Army Medical Museum possessed nearly 3,000 specimens."

"At all events he was very happy to announce to Doctor

Yarrow in 1874 that he had received from Dr. Henry McEldrey [sic], the Post Surgeon at Fort Klamath, Oregon, the skulls of the Modoc murderers, [viz.,] Captain Jack, 'Shacknasty Jim' (sic), 'Steamboat Frank' (sic) and others. Dr. Yarrow was equally happy because these murderers had killed his friend and former commanding officer, Captain Evan Thomas, 4th Artillery." (Doctor Kober later spent duty time at Camp Bidwell in extreme northeast California and at Camp McDermit on the Oregon-Nevada boundary line).

Quoting from a letter sent from F.N. Setzler, head curator, Department of Anthropology, Smithsonian Institution, to Kenneth McLeod, Jr., dated January 26, 1949: "Your inquiry of Jan. 9 concerning the final resting place of the bodies of four Indian leaders executed at Fort Klamath in 1873 has been referred to Dr. M. T. Newman of our division of physical anthropology.

"Dr. Newman states that although there is no mention of the disposition of the bodies in the biographies published in the 'Handbook of American Indians', it is probable that the skulls of these four Indians are now in the national museum.

"An old catalogue of specimens in the Army Medical Museum lists SEVEN Modoc crania [emphasis supplied]. Four of these were received from Surgeon H. McElderry, U.S. Army, Fort Klamath, in 1873.

"The names of the Indians are not mentioned in the records, so that their skulls cannot be identified. But the circumstantial evidence points to their being the skulls of Captain Jack, Schonchin John, Black Jim, and Boston Charley."

Crania numbers five and six were probably those of the two Klamath — not Modoc — chiefs hanged without trial by Lt. Colonel Charles S. Drew in the fall of 1863 — George (Kiluamch, brother of Poos Kiyou — Allen David) and Skookum John, and the seventh could have been the skull of either Red Blanket or Beaded Hat, both Klamaths.

The letter also stated that the Army Medical Museum made no mention of skeletons from local Indians preserved there. It continued, "In all probability, the bodies were buried, possibly at the fort after the execution, and only the skulls sent to the museum".

Many reports, both military and newspaper, describe the six newly dug graves. Six Modoc Indians had been convicted by the Military Commission. From the findings of the Military Commission all six of the Modoc Indians were fully aware that their destiny was to be death by hanging. Yet in an executive order dated Sept. 10, 1873 from President Ulysses Grant, the sentences of Barncho and Slolux were commuted to life imprisonment in the military prison at Alcatraz Island in San Francisco Bay. But, the word was silence, and commutation was not made known to the two Indians until about 2 A.M. on the morning of October 3, 1873, the date of the executions, by the Officer of the Day, Lt. Sydney W. Taylor, Battery B, Fourth Artillery Regiment.

After the grisly spectacle of four simultaneous hangings and whatever dismemberment Dr. McElderry may have committed, four caskets were lowered into grave numbers (from the south) two, three, four, and five. Earth was then shovelled in to close all six graves, numbers one and six having been intended for Barncho and Slolux.

Examination of the graves today yields the following: Graves two, three, four, and five, shown as mounds in Lt. Parke's watercolor are now sodded depressions, the lowest points of which are several inches (in the order of four to six) deep. It appears that the lowest contents of the graves, i.e., their caskets and corpses, decayed and atrophied, respectively, thus allowing the soil overburden to sink.

Soil surface at grave number two, that containing the remains of Captain Jack, is depressed the same amount as grave three (as the original headboard read, Schonchiss), or grave four (Black Jim), or grave five (Boston Charley). Conclusion: If Captain Jack's body was stolen from grave two, as has been alleged, then there are no bodies in three, four, or five. Grass cover at graves one and six should not have sunk as much as the other four because the graves contained only soil, subject only to compaction and not decomposition. Nor have they.

One further aspect should be mentioned. When the 50 foot by 150 foot log stockade was built, it was located 200 yards west of the guard house. When the graves were dug in

early October, they were located east of the stockade, west of
the guardhouse, and about 20 feet north of the line
connecting the two. The three features were clustered rather
closely together, considering the size of the military reservation. This arrangement eased the job of guarding all
prisoners and, quite sadistically, impressed the Indians with
all the ignominy directed at them. ("...put in their coffins
and buried, as I [William Bunker] have before stated, in
close proximity to the post guardhouse where the sentinel, in
death as well as life, will watch over them and take good care
that they are not disturbed...")

If Captain Jack's body was stolen (as has been alleged) in
a ghoulish enterprise on that first evening, a conspiracy of
humongous proportions was carried out in full view of
reporters, Indian captives, guard details, and most important, in front of those Indians permitted freedom from the
stockade, Scarface Charley and the four "Bloodhounds" —
Hooker Jim, Bogus Charley, Shacknasty Jim, and Steamboat Frank. Hardly seems possible.

Before leaving the subject, a corollary quotation can be
taken from the Kober volume: "(at Alcatraz)...It was at this
station that the writer observed cases of scrofulous Adenitis
for the first time in two Indian warriors who were implicated
in the assassination of General Canby during the Modoc
War. These cases responded favorably to hypodermic
injections of carbolated glycerine and a hygienic and dietetic
regime." Barncho died in Alcatraz of that affliction and
Slolux was pardoned to join the Modocs in exile in Indian
Territory, now Oklahoma. He changed his name to George
Denny.

One last note to record the location of the multiple
gallows: Some written reports have located the massive
gallows north of the fort, somewhere west of the hospital.
Kingsbury's return places the gallows both west and south of
the guardhouse. This writer has discussed the location with
two friends from Wood River valley. Both had had birthdates
circa 1900. They were J. Emmett Sisemore and L. Orth
Sisemore. Both are now deceased. Their mother and father
were among the early settlers in that beautiful valley.

Both men were very explicit (in substance): "It stood for

a long time and was near the barn..." "Near the barn" is just where Kingsbury had it. Of course the scaffold predates the barn by many years. The Sisemores made it clear that the scaffold was still evident at the same time as was the barn. Thus, no poles or timbers in the barn should show any marks by adze or axe not consistent with the present structure of the barn. None do.

Lt. Parke's watercolor shows the scaffold as it was when he saw it. Note that the "non-moveable platform or stanchion" and the "moveable drop" were gone. Probably a safety measure.

No parts of the original fort now remain other than isolated clumps of stone which were used as foundations. Some twenty-five years ago, two feed troughs for cattle were inside the corral enclosure of the Zumbruns. The "logs" used in constructing the troughs had been hewn square and were notched at the ends (and in some, at intermediate points). They were paced out to be about 32-34 feet long and were about 6" or 7" square. Quite clearly they were salvage from the original guardhouse. A recent search for further evidence of either the guardhouse timbers or any parts of the gallows turned up but one piece of squared log about 12 feet long, serving as a fence cornerpost. Near midpoint is a very clean mortise where there is no need for one. All else is gone and all that remains is the beautiful little Klamath County park "blooming green under the summer sun".

This article should never have had to be written. Poor communication, immense greed, and stoical adversity exacerbated what could have been a passable arrangement of mutual coexistence to a cruel, bloody, and expensive tragedy. A race of people exterminated. Doubtless the echo will remain forever.

APPENDIX B

PROCEEDINGS OF A MILITARY COMMISSION

CONVENED AT

FORT KLAMATH, OREGON,

FOR THE

TRIAL OF MODOC PRISONERS.

LIEUT. COL. W. L. ELLIOTT, PRESIDENT.
MAJOR H. P. CURTIS, JUDGE-ADVOCATE.

JULY, 1873.

OFFICIAL COPY OF THE TRIAL OF THE MODOC INDIANS.
J. HOLT,
Judge-Advocate General.

PROCEEDINGS OF A MILITARY COMMISSION.

⁊ ————

Proceedings of a Military Commission convened at Fort Klamath, Oregon, by virtue of the following order :

[Special Field Orders No. 1.]

HEADQUARTERS DEPARTMENT OF THE COLUMBIA,
"In the field" Fort Klamath, Oregon, June 30, 1873.

A Military Commission is hereby appointed to meet at Fort Klamath, Oregon, on Tuesday, July 1, 1873, at 10 o'clock a. m., or as soon thereafter as practicable, for the trial of the Modoc chief known as Captain Jack, and such other Indian captives as may be properly brought before it.

Detail for the commission.—Lieut. Col. Washington L. Elliott, First Cavalry; Capt. John Mendenhall, Fourth Artillery; Capt. Henry C. Hasbrouck, Fourth Artillery; Capt. Robert Pollock, Twenty-first Infantry; Second Lieut. George W. Kingsbury, Twelfth Infantry.

Maj. H. P. Curtis, Judge-Advocate U. S. A., is appointed Judge-Advocate of the commission.

No other officers than those named can be assembled without manifest injury to the service. Should any of the officers named in the detail be unable to attend, the commission will nevertheless proceed to, and continue the business before it, provided the number present be not less than the minimum prescribed by law. The commission will sit without regard to hours.

JEF. C. DAVIS,
Brevet Major-General Commanding.

FORT KLAMATH, OREGON,
July 1, 1873—10 o'clock a. m.

The commission met pursuant to the foregoing order.

Present, Lieut. Col. Washington L. Elliott, First Cavalry; Capt. John Mendenhall, Fourth Artillery; Capt. Henry C. Hasbrouck, Fourth Artillery; Capt. Robert Pollock, Twenty-first Infantry; Second Lieut. George Kingsbury, Twelfth Infantry; Maj. H. P. Curtis, Judge-Advocate.

The judge-advocate then stated to the commission that in consequence of the brief period of time he had had since arriving at the post he had been unable to prepare a case; and suggested an adjournment for some days. The commission thereupon decided to adjourn until Saturday next, the 5th instant, at 10 o'clock a. m.

Adjourned at 10½ a. m.

H. P. CURTIS,
Judge-Advocate Commission.

————

SECOND DAY.

FORT KLAMATH, *July* 5, 1873.

The commission met at 10 a. m., pursuant to adjournment.

Present, all of the members of the commission, the judge-advocate, and prisoners.

The proceedings of the last meeting were read and approved.

The judge-advocate then read before the commission the order convening the commission, (see page 1 of this record,) which is interpreted to the prisoners.

The commission then proceeded to the trial of the prisoners: Captain Jack, Schonchis, Black Jim, Boston Charley, Barncho, (*alias* One-Eyed Jim,) and Sloluck, Modoc Indian captives, who being called before the commission, and having heard the order convening it read, it being interpreted to them, were severally asked if they had any objection to any member present named in the order, to which they severally replied in the negative.

The members of the commission were then duly sworn by the judge-advocate; and the judge-advocate was then duly sworn by the president of the commission; all of which oaths were administered and interpreted in the presence of the prisoners.

The judge-advocate asked the authority of the commission to employ T. F. Riddle and wife as interpreters at $10 a day, which authority was given by the commission.

T. F. Riddle and wife (Toby) were then duly sworn to the faithful performance of their duty in the interpretation of the evidence and proceedings as required, in the presence of the prisoners, which oath was interpreted to the prisoners.

The judge-advocate then presented to the commission E. S. Belden, the official short-hand reporter, who was then duly sworn to the faithful performance of his duty; which oath was duly interpreted to the prisoners.

The prisoners were then severally asked by the judge-advocate if they desired to introduce counsel; to which they severally replied in the negative; and that they had been unable to procure any.

The prisoners were then severally duly arraigned on the following charges and specifications:

Charges and specifications preferred against certain Modoc Indians commonly known and called as Captain Jack, Schonchis, Boston Charley, Black Jim, Barncho, alias One-Eyed Jim, and Sloluck, alias Cok.

CHARGE 1. "Murder, in violation of the laws of war."

Specification 1. "In this, that they, Indians called and commonly known as Captain Jack, Schonchis, Boston Charley, Black Jim, Barncho, *alias* One-Eyed Jim, and Sloluck, *alias* Cok, members of a certain band of Indians known as the Modocs, which band, including the prisoners above named, was, at the time and place hereinafter alleged, engaged in open and flagrant war with the United States, under the chief command of said Captain Jack, did, as representatives of said Modoc band, meet, under a flag of truce and suspension of hostilities, Brig. Gen. E. R. S. Canby, U. S. A., commanding the Department of the Columbia, and certain peace commissioners on the part of the said United States, namely, Eleazur Thomas, A. B. Meacham, and L. S. Dyer, citizens of the United States, all representing the Government of the United States, for the agreed and professed purpose of discussing and arranging terms upon which hostilities existing between the United States and said band should cease, and did thereupon, in wanton violation of said flag of truce, and treacherously disregarding the obligations imposed by said truce under the laws of war, willfully, feloniously, and of malice aforethought, kill and murder said Brigadier-General Canby.

"All this at or near the lava-beds, so-called, situated near Tule Lake, in the State of California, on or about the 11th day of April, A. D. 1873."

Specification 2. "In this, that they, Indians called and commonly known as Captain Jack, Schonchis, Boston Charley, Black Jim, Barncho, *alias* One-Eyed Jim, and Sloluck, *alias* Cok, members of a certain band of Indians known as the Modocs, which band, including the prisoners above named, was, at the time and place hereinafter alleged, engaged in open and flagrant war with the United States, under the chief command of said Captain Jack, did, as representatives of said Modoc band, meet under a flag of truce and suspension of hostilities Brig. Gen. E. R. S. Canby, U. S. A., commanding Military Department of the Columbia, and certain peace commissioners on the part of the United States, namely, Eleazur Thomas, A. B. Meacham, and L. S. Dyer, citizens of the United States, all representing the Government of the United States, for the agreed and professed purpose of discussing and arranging terms upon which hostilities existing between the United States and said bands should cease, and did thereupon, in wanton violation of the sacred character of said flag of truce, and treacherously disregarding the obligations imposed by such truce, under the laws of war, willfully, feloniously, and of their malice aforethought, kill and murder said Eleazur Thomas, one of the peace commissioners aforesaid.

"All this at or near the lava-beds, so-called, situated near Tule Lake, in the State of California, on or about the 11th day of April, A. D. 1873."

CHARGE 2. "Assault with intent to kill, in violation of the laws of war."

Specification 1. "In this, that they, Indians, called and commonly known as Captain Jack, Schonchis, Boston Charley, Black Jim, Barncho, *alias* One Eyed Jim, and Sloluck, *alias* Cok, members of a certain band of Indians known as the Modocs, which band, including the prisoners above named, was, at the time and place hereinafter alleged, engaged in open and flagrant war with the United States, under the chief command of said Captain Jack, did, as representatives of said Modoc band, meet, under a flag of truce and suspension of hostilities, Brig. Gen. E. R. S. Canby, U. S. A., commanding the Department of the Columbia, and certain peace commissioners on the part of the United States, namely, Eleazur Thomas, A. B. Meacham, and L. S. Dyer, citizens, all representing the Government of the United States, for the agreed and professed purpose of discussing and arranging terms upon which hostilities existing between the United States and said band should cease; and did thereupon, in wanton violation of the sacred character of said flag of truce, and treacherously disregarding the obligations imposed by such truce under the laws of war, feloniously make an assault with deadly weapons upon the said A. B. Meacham, then and there feloniously, willfully, and of malice aforethought to kill and murder, and did inflict upon the body of the said Meacham divers severe and dangerous wounds.

"All this at or near the lava-beds, so-called, situated near Tule Lake, in the State of California, on or about the 11th day of April, A. D. 1873."

Specification 2. "In this, that they, Indians called and commonly known as Captain Jack, Schonchis, Boston Charley, Black Jim, Barncho, *alias* One Eyed Jim, and Sloluck, *alias* Cok, members of a certain band of Indians known as Modocs, which band, including the prisoners above named, was, at the time and place hereinafter alleged, engaged in open and flagrant war with the United States under the chief command of said Captain Jack, did, as representatives of said Modoc band, meet, under a flag of truce and suspension of hostilities, Brig. Gen. E. R. S. Canby, U. S. A., and certain peace commissioners on the part of the United States, namely, Eleazur Thomas, A. B. Meacham, and L. S. Dyer, citizens, all representing the Government of the United States, for the agreed and professed purpose of discussing and arranging terms upon which hostilities existing between the United States and said band should cease; and did then and there, in wanton violation of said flag of truce, and treacherously disregarding the obligations imposed by such truce under the laws of war, feloniously make an assault with deadly weapons upon the said Dyer, commissioner as aforesaid, with an intent him, said Dyer, then and there feloniously, willfully, and of their malice aforethought to kill and murder.

"All this at or near the lava-beds, so-called, situated near Tule Lake, in the State of California, on or about the 11th day of April, 1873."

To which the prisoners severally pleaded as follows :
To first specification, first charge, " Not guilty."
To second specification, first charge, " Not guilty."
To first charge, " Not guilty."
To first specification, second charge, " Not guilty."
To second specification, second charge, " Not guilty."
To second charge, " Not guilty."

T. F. RIDDLE, a citizen and witness for the prosecution, being duly sworn by the judge-advocate, testified as follows :

Question by judge-advocate. Were you present at the meeting of the commissioners and General Canby, referred to in the charges and specifications just read ?—Answer. Yes, sir.

Q. On what day was it ?—A. On the 11th of April, I believe, as near as I can recollect.

Q. Were the prisoners at the bar present on that occasion ?—A. Yes, sir.

Q. You identify them all ?—A. Yes, sir; I identify all but Barncho and Sloluck. I saw them, but I didn't know them. They were some 75 yards behind me; they came up behind.

Q. Is Captain Jack the principal man in this Modoc band ?—A. Yes, sir.

Q. What is he? Describe him.—A. He is a chief amongst them. He has been a chief since 1861, I believe.

Q. What position did Schonchis hold among the Modocs ?—A. I never knew him to be anything more than just a common man amongst them until, within the last year, he has been classed as Captain Jack's sub-chief, I believe; they call it a " Sergeant."

Q. Black Jim ?—A. He has been classed as one of his watchmen, they call them.

Q. Boston Charley ?—A. He is nothing more than a high private.

Q. Barncho ?—A. He is not anything.

Q. Sloluck ?—A. He is not anything.

Q. Are they all Modocs ?—A. Yes, sir; they are classed as Modocs, one of them is a Rock Indian, or a " Combaterash."

Q. Were they all present at this meeting of the 11th of April ?—A. Yes, sir. Barncho and Sloluck was not in the council. They came up after the firing commenced.

Q. What connection did you have with the peace commissioners from the beginning ?—A. I was employed by General Gillem to interpret, and then from that I was turned over to the peace commissioners ; but I acted as interpreter all of the time—all through their councils.

Q. Did you ever receive any information which led you to suppose it was a dangerous matter for the commissioners to interview these men? —A. Yes, sir; the first that I learned was when I stopped at Fairchild's. They agreed to meet the wagons out between Little Klamath and the lava-bed, and all of them come in, women and children. They said Captain Jack sent word that if General Canby would send his wagons out there, they would send his women and children in.

Q. Were you present at the killing of General Canby and Mr. Meacham?—A. Yes, sir.

Q. Had you received any information which led you to think that it was dangerous?—A. Yes, sir, I had; my woman, some week or ten days before that, went to carry a message into Jack's cave where he was living, and there was an Indian called William—he followed her after she started from home back to camp, he followed her out.

Q. How do you know this?—A. My woman told me.

Q. In consequence of some information which you received, what did you then do? Did you speak to the commissioners about it?—A. Yes, sir; I told them I received information, and then I went to the peace commissioners and told them it was dangerous to go out there any more to meet them, and I advised them not to go. While I was at Fairchild's, this Hooka Jim, he came there and took me out one side and told me, "If you ever come with them peace commissioners to meet us any more and I come to you and push you to one side, you stand back one side and we won't hurt you, but will murder them."

Q. Do I understand you to say you then cautioned the commissioners?—A. Yes; I told them of it.

Q. What did you say?—A. I told them what Hooka Jim told me; and I said I didn't think it was of any use to try to make peace with those Indians without going to the lava-beds, right where they were. I said, "I think the best way, if you want to make peace with them, is to give them a good licking, and then make peace."

Q. Did you tell them what Hooka Jim said?—A. Yes, sir; and at another time, I believe it was the very next time after we were out in the lava-beds—after General Gillem had moved over to the lava-beds— we met, and Hooka Jim came to me after we got to the ground where we were to hold our council, and he took hold of me and said, "You come out here and sit down;" and he pushed me as he said he would. I said "No."

Q. When was this?—A. I don't remember the date; it was some time in March.

A. The first or second meeting?—A. The first meeting after Hooka Jim had told me this at Fairchild's.

Q. Were they the same, or other commissioners?—A. It was General Canby, Dr. Thomas, and Mr. Dyer, and Judge Rosbourgh, I believe, was along, if I am not mistaken; I won't be positive. Hooka Jim came to me and caught hold of me, and pushed me one side, and said, "You stand out here." I told him "No;" that I had to go and talk and interpret for them; and my woman here spoke up to him to behave himself, and not go doing anything while he was there; and he then said, "Well, go and sit down."

Q. Did you visit the lava-beds before the massacre; and, if so, did you go alone, or with some one else?—A. The first time I went in there was with Squire Steele. Fairchild ——

Q. (Interrupting.) Very shortly before the massacre, did you?—A. Well, I was in there.

Q. State why you went in there.—A. I was in there on the 10th of

April. My woman and me went in there, and took a written message in there from the peace commissioners. I read and interpreted it to Captain Jack, and I told him then, after I interpreted it to him, that I gave him a notice; and I told him to bring it the next day when he met the commissioners, to bring it with him. He threw it on the ground, and he said he was no white man; he could not read, and had no use for it. He would meet the commissioners close to his camp—about a mile beyond what they called the peace-tent. He said he would meet them there and nowhere else.

Q. A mile nearer the lava-beds than the peace-tent ?—A. Yes; he said that was all he had to say then. I could hear them talking around, and sort of making light of the peace commissioners—as much as to say they didn't care for them.

Q. What was the tenor of this message you say you read ?—A. It was a statement that they wished to hold a council with them at the peace-tent next day, to have a permanent settlement of the difficulties between the whites and the Indians; they wanted to make peace, and move them off to some warm climate, where they could live like white people.

Q. Where is that note you carried ?—A. It is lost.

Q. Did Captain Jack say anything about arms in reference to the meeting ?—A. Yes, sir; he said he would meet them five men without arms, and he would do the same—he would not take any arms with him.

Q. That he would meet them at the place he fixed—one mile nearer the lava-beds ?—A. Yes, sir; one mile nearer the lava-beds.

Q. Five men, without arms, and he would also go without arms ?—A. Yes, sir.

The COURT. Five, including himself ?—A. Yes, sir.

The JUDGE-ADVOCATE. What did he say about the proposition to move him from the lava-beds ?—A. He said he knew no other country only this, and he did not want to leave it.

Q. Did he say anything about a desire for peace ?—A. Yes; he said if they would move the soldiers all away he would make peace then, and live right there where he was, and would not pester anybody else; he would live peaceably there.

Q. Was Captain Jack alone in this interview when you talked with him ?—A. No, sir; these other men were around with him, sitting down.

Q. These prisoners here now ?—A. Some of them.

Q. Did he do all or only a part of the talking ?—A. That evening he done all of the talking—that is, he was the only one that had anything to say to me in regard to this affair.

Q. Did you see anything there which led you to suppose that they intended hostilities ?—A. Yes, sir; I did; I saw that they had forted up all around his cave.

Q. Did they seem to be well provisioned ?—A. They had just been killing several beeves there that day.

Q. Which of these men were there at the time ?—A. Boston was there—most all of these that are here.

Q. Can't you name them ?—A. There was Boston, Black Jim was there, and Barncho; I don't remember whether Schonchis was there or not at the time the conversation was going on.

Q. Did you go back to the commissioners then ?—A. Yes, sir.

Q. State the facts about it. State what followed after your return to the commissioners ?—A. I went back and went into the peace commissioners' tent with Jack's message that he would meet them five unarmed, and he would do the same; he would have five men with himself, and go without arms; and I told him they were forted all around there, and they had been killing beef; and I thought it was useless to try to make peace any longer; and if Captain Jack would not agree to meet at the tent, and if I were in their places I would not meet them any more.

Q. What did the commissioners then reply or decide upon? What decision did they come to?—A. They held a council between themselves. I was not at their council.

Q. Was your visit the day before the assassination?—A. Yes, sir; I seen General Canby that evening; and I told him I had a proposition to make to him. He was out, and I met him, and he wanted to know what it was; I told him that if I was in his place, if I calculated on meeting them Indians, I would send twenty-five or thirty men near the place were I expected to hold the council, to secrete themselves in the rocks there; that they would stand a good show to catch them, if they undertook to do anything that was wrong. General Canby said that that would be too much of an insult to Captain Jack; that if they knew of that they *might* do an injury then; he would not do that.

Q. Did you hear him say that?—A. Yes.

Q. Did they determine to meet him, or not?—A. They sent to me the next morning, then, to come down to the peace commissioners' tent.

Q. Was Captain Jack informed that they would not go to that place one mile nearer?—A. Yes, sir; Bogus Charley went in that evening before the murder, right ahead of me, into General Gillem's camp and staid all night. He staid at my camp, and the next morning the peace commissioners decided that they would not meet Captain Jack in this place where he wanted to meet them, and sent a message out by Bogus and Boston for them to meet him at the peace commissioners' tent, the peace tent, and they were gone about an hour; and they came back again and said that Captain Jack was there with five men.

Q. (Interrupting.) You heard it?—A. Yes.

Q. Jack was to meet them where; he was where?—A. He was at the peace-tent.

Q. Captain Jack sent back a message then by Bogus and Boston that he would meet them at the peace-tent with five men?—A. Yes, sir; but they were not armed, and he wanted the peace commissioners to go without arms.

Q. He sent that message, and you heard it?—A. Yes, sir.

Q. What advice, if any, did you then give the commissioners?—A. My woman and me went down to the peace commissioners' tent and she went to Mr. Meacham; I saw her myself at the first, though I told him not to meet them.

Q. Were you at the peace commissioners' tent when you gave them this advice?—A. The peace commissioners' tent in General Gillem's camp.

Q. Not the large peace-tent?—A. No; the peace commissioners' tent. He wanted to know why, and I told him they intended to murder them, and that they might do it that day if everything was not right; and my woman went and took hold of Mr. Meacham and told him not to go; and held on to him and cried. She said " Meacham, don't you go!"—I heard her say so myself—" for they might kill you to-day; they may kill all of you to-day;" and Dr. Thomas, he came up and told me that I ought to put my trust in God; that God Almighty would not let any such body of men be hurt that was on as good a mission as that. I told him at the time that he might trust in God, but that I didn't trust any in them Indians.

140   MODOC WAR.

Q. Did any of the other commissioners make any reply?—A. Mr. Meacham said that he knew there was danger, and he believed me, every word I said, and he believed the woman, and so did Mr. Dyer. He said he believed it; and he said that he felt like he was going to his grave. I went then to General Canby and asked him if General Gillem was going out. He said "no." I said, I want your commissioners then to go to General Gillem's tent with me.

Q. Did they go?—A. Yes, sir.

Q. Was Toby with you?—A. No, sir; she was not with me then; she was standing holding her horse.

Q. State what occurred at General Gillem's tent.—A. We went down with Mr. Meacham, General Canby, Dyer, and Dr. Thomas; and General Canby walked down with us. General Canby did not go into the tent, but the other three went in; that is, Mr. Dyer, Meacham, and Dr. Thomas, and I went in to General Gillem and said, "General Gillem, these men are going out to hold council with them Indians to-day, and I don't believe it is safe. If there is anything happens to them, I don't want no blame laid on me hereafter, because I don't think it is safe for them to go, and after it is over I don't want nothing laid on me;" said I, "I am not much afraid of the Indians; but I will go before I will be called a coward."

Q. State what followed then.—A. Well, before we got through the conversation there, General Gillem—that is, there was not anything more—and then General Gillem gave a big laugh, and said if the Indians done anything, that he would take care of them, and we started out, and General Canby and Dr. Thomas started on ahead; Mr. Meacham and he went to Toby, (my wife,) and asked her if she thought the Indians would kill him, and she said, "I have told you all I *can* tell you;" she said, "they may kill you to-day, and they may not."

Q. You heard this?—A. Yes. "But," says she, "don't go." By that time General Canby and Dr. Thomas had got some one hundred yards ahead of us. Bogus Charley walked out; General Canby and Dr. Thomas walked; Mr. Dyer, Meacham, and Toby rode horseback.

The COURT. Did Bogus Charley walk out with you?—A. Yes; him and me were behind.

The JUDGE ADVOCATE. Where was Boston Charley at this time?—A. If I am not mistaken, he was with General Canby and Dr. Thomas.

Q. Did you finally arrive at the peace-tent?—A. Yes, sir.

Q. And whom did you find there?—A. I found Captain Jack, Schonchis, and Black Jim, (Ellen's man,) who is dead, they say, Schacknasty Jim, and Hooka Jim.

Q. Were there any others?—A. There were no others; well, Boston, he went out with us, and Bogus Charley; there were eight of them there.

Q. Eight were there in the party?—A. In the council; yes, sir.

Q. What took place after you met these Modocs whom you have named—between the commissioners and they?—A. Well, we all sat down around a little fire we had there, built, I suppose, some 20 or 30 feet from the peace-tent. There was some sage-brush thrown on, and we were all sitting around the little fire, and General Canby gave them all a cigar apiece, and they all sat around there and smoked a few minutes, and then they went to talking; General Canby, I think, though I won't be certain, made the first speech, and told them that he had been dealing with the Indians for some thirty years, and he had come there to make peace with them and to talk good; and that whatever he promised to give them that he would see that they got; and if they would come and go out with him, that he would take them to a good country, and fix them up so that they could live like white people.

Q. Did you interpret all of this to the Indians ?—A. Yes, sir.

Q. So that they understood it?—A. Yes, my wife and me did together.

Q. Was that the summary of General Canby's speech ?—A. That was about the substance of his speech, with the exception that he told them that he had a couple of Indian names; that he had taken Indians on to a reservation once before, and that they all liked him, and had given him a name.

Q. General Canby said that?—A. Yes. They sat and laughed about it. I disremember the name now.

Q. Do you know who spoke next ?—A. Mr. Meacham spoke next, and he told them he had come there to make peace with them; that their Great Father from Washington had sent him there to make peace, and wipe out all of the blood that had been shed, and to take them to some country where they could have good homes, and be provided with blankets, food, and the like.

Q. That was Mr. Meacham's speech ?—A. Yes, sir. Dr. Thomas, he said a few words. He said the Great Father had sent him there to make peace with them, and to wipe out all of the blood that had been shed, and not to have any more trouble, to move them out of this country here—that is the place where they were stopping.

Q. Mr. Riddle, do you know whether the lava-beds are in the State of California?—A. Yes, sir; it is. I could not be certain what the extent of it is; it may be possible a small portion of it is in Oregon.

Q. How near to the lava-beds was General Gillem's camp?—A. It was about two miles and a half from Jack's stronghold.

Q. How near to the lava-beds was the peace-tent ?—A. It was right on the edge of it.

Q. What distance from General Gillem's quarters or camp ?—A. I think about three-quarters of a mile.

Q. Did any Modocs reply to those speeches ?—A. Captain Jack, he spoke.

Q. What did he say; can you remember ?—A. Yes, I can recollect some of what he said. He said that he didn't want to leave this country here; that he knew no other country than this; that he didn't want to leave here; and that he had given up Lost River; and he asked for Cottonwood and Willow Creek; that is over near Fairchild's.

Q. Is Cottonwood Creek the same as Hot Creek ?—A. They are two different creeks.

Q. What did he mean by giving up Lost River?—A. He said there was where the fight had taken place; and that he didn't want to have anything more to do there. He said he thought that was what the fight took place about—that country there; he said the whites wanted it.

Q. What fight do you refer to?—A. The first fight, where Major Jackson went down to bring them down on to the reservation; that was in November, 1872.

Q. Did Captain Jack demand Willow Creek and Cottonwood Creeks? A. Yes, sir.

Q. That is, the land around this place ?—A. Yes.

Q. To live on?—A. Yes, sir; he wanted a reservation there.

Q. Then what was said, or what occurred ?—A. Mr. Meacham, then he made another speech, and he told Captain Jack: "Jack, let us talk like men, and not like children," and he sort of hit him on the knee or shoulder—probably hit him on the shoulder once or twice, or tapped him—he said, " Let us talk like men, and not talk like children." He said, " You are a man that has common sense; isn't there any other place that will do you except Willow Creek and Cottonwood?" And Mr. Meacham was speaking rather loud, and Schonchis told him to hush—told him in Indian to hush; that he could talk a straight talk; to let him talk. Just as Schonchis said that, Captain Jack rose up and stepped back, sort of in behind Dyer's horse. I was interpreting for Schonchis, and I was not noticing Jack. He stepped a few steps out to one side, and I seen him put his hand in his bosom like——

Q. (Interrupting) Did you perceive as soon as you got there that these men were armed?—A. Yes, sir; I did; I could see some of them were.

Q. In what way did you observe that?—A. I saw these sticking out of their clothes.

Q. You saw what?—A. They were revolvers.

Q. Did Captain Jack at this interview represent this band?—A. Yes, sir.

Q. And these other men listened and appeared to concur?—A. Yes, sir.

Q. Were they there as representatives of the band?—A. Yes, sir; I suppose they were.

Q. You say Captain Jack got up and went to the rear, and you saw him put his hand to his breast?—A. Yes, sir.

Q. What then occurred?—A. Well, he stepped back and came right up in front of General Canby, and said, in Indian, "All ready, boys"—At we—that is, "All ready," and the cap bursted, and before you could crack your finger he fired.

Q. You saw this?—A. Yes, sir; and after the cap bursted, before you could crack your finger, he fired and struck General Canby under the eye, and the ball came out here, (showing—in the neck, under the chin.) I jumped and ran then, and never stopped to look back any more. I saw General Canby fall over, and I expected he was killed, and I jumped and ran with all my might. I never looked back but once, and when I looked back Mr. Meacham was down and my woman was down, and there was an Indian standing over Mr. Meacham and another Indian standing over her, and some two or three coming up to Mr. Meacham. Mr. Meacham was sort of lying down this way, (showing,) and had one of his hands sticking out.

Q. You saw General Canby fall, you say?—A. Yes, sir.

Q. Did he continue to lie where he fell?—A. He was not when they found him; he was about thirty or forty yards from there. I did not see him get up.

Q. As soon as Captain Jack fired what then occurred?—A. They commenced firing all around. I could not tell who was firing except Schonchis here; I seen him firing at Mr. Meacham, but the others were kind of up in behind me, and they were firing, and I did not turn around to look to see who it was. I thought it was warm times there.

Q. Did any other Indians come up?—A. Just as the firing commenced I seen two Indians coming up packing their guns.

Q. What do you mean by "packing their guns?"—A. They were carrying them along in their arms.

Q. How many had each man?—A. I could not tell; it looked like they had some two or three apiece.

Q. Can you identify those men?—A. No, sir, I cannot. I did not stop to look to see who they were. I saw they were Indians.

Q. Did you see General Canby at any time afterward ?—A. Yes, sir; I seen him that afternoon.

Q. In what condition was he ?—A. He was laying in his tent, dead, with his clothing all taken off of him.

Q. Did you see the wounds ?—A. I seen only one; yes, I seen two wounds.

Q. Did you see Dr. Thomas afterward ?—A. Yes, sir.

Q. In what condition was he?—A. He was dead, and lying in his tent.

Q. Describe the wounds upon him.—A. I saw a wound in his head, and I don't recollect—he was kind of covered over—I don't recollect whether I seen any other wounds.

Q. You knew it to be his body ?—A. Yes, sir.

Q. You recognized him ?—Yes, sir.

Q. And you recognized General Canby ?—A. Yes, sir.

Q. When you ran were you not pursued ?—A. Yes, sir; there were three Indians running after me.

Q. How long was that after the first firing by Captain Jack ?—A. It wasn't but a few seconds. I guess I must have got some—well, I didn't turn around to see who it was shooting at me. I could see the dust flying ahead of me from the bullets, and I did not turn around until I had come one hundred yards or more; then I just turned my head around and seen three, and just as I turned again one ball came by my ear here and grazed it a little.

Q. You cannot say who those men were that pursued you ?—A. No, I cannot say only from hearsay.

Q. Did you see Mr. Meacham after the massacre ?—A. Yes, sir.

Q. In what condition was he ?—A. He was pretty badly wounded. He was shot some two or three times. He had a shot that went up across his nose like and came out here, (above and between the eyes.) He had one of his fingers shot about off, and a wound of one of his arms; I don't remember which.

Q. Was he in good health when he went to the meeting ?—A. Yes, sir.

Q. He was not wounded ?—A. No, sir; he was not wounded.

Q. Had you, during your abode with the commissioners, seen any hostilities between the United States forces and the Indian forces ?—A. No, sir; I had not.

Q. Had there been a suspension of arms, then, while you were there ?—A. Yes, sir.

Q. There was no fighting going on while you was there ?—A. No, sir.

Q. How long were you there ?—A. I went there the 11th of February, and I left there the 11th of May, I believe.

Q. Was there or not a flag sent out by Captain Jack, inviting this meeting ?—A. There was no flag sent, just merely men came.

Q. Messengers were sent instead of a flag ?—A. Yes, sir.

Q. I understood you to say it was Captain Jack himself who told you that they would go five in number, without arms ?—A. Yes, sir.

Q. And that they expected the commissioners to do the same ?—A. Yes, sir.

The judge-advocate then asked the prisoners severally if they desired to cross-examine the witness, to which they replied in the negative.

Question by the COURT: Did Bogus Charley or not infer to you that the peace commissioners were going to be killed that day ?—A. No, sir; he did not.

Q. He did not repeat to you that he wished you to stand aside, then?—A. No, sir; he didn't that day. Bogus Charley never did.

Q. Didn't I understand you that Bogus Charley had told you that when he pushed you aside ——A. (Interrupting.) No, sir; Hooka Jim.

Q. You say that when Captain Jack went behind the horse he put his hand in his shirt this way, (showing,) and then he came back up before General Canby. Did you see a weapon in his hand?—A. I only saw him have his hand in his shirt-bosom.

Q. You didn't see him have a pistol?—A. No, sir; not until he jerked it out.

Q. Did you see the pistol in his hand at any time?—A. Yes; I seen it when the pistol snapped, and I seen it when he fired, and I seen General Canby fall.

Q. When General Canby was making his speech, and said that he had dwelt among the Indians for thirty years, did he use that term, "dwelt among the Indians," or that he had been among the Indians at different times, for some thirty years, as an officer?—A. That he had been—the way he spoke was, that he had been engaged in removing Indians from different places to reservations; that he had moved the Indians; that the Indians sort of liked him; that they hated to leave the country, but that he had removed them, and they all liked him afterward; that they all shook hands with him, and gave him a name. I disremember the name they gave him.

Q. You used the word "dwelt;" you now say he had "*been*" among the Indians in different countries acting in the capacity of an officer?—A. Yes, sir.

Question by judge-advocate. Mr. Riddle, was anything done by the commissioners, or any one or more of them, to give occasion for this attack upon them at the hands of the Indians?—A. No, sir; not that I know of.

Q. Did you see anything?—A. I saw nothing.

Q. So far as you saw, then, it was without justification?—A. Yes, sir; it was without justification.

Question by the COURT. I would like to inquire if Captain Jack is the only Indian at the bar of trial that you can actually identify now as having discharged a pistol or gun at the peace commissioners at the time.—A. Schonchis, here. I saw him shoot, because he was pretty nigh between Captain Jack and I.

Q. Captain Jack and Schonchis are the only two men you can speak positively of, of your own knowledge?—A. Yes, sir.

Question by the judge-advocate. Can you say what was the purpose of the peace commissioners in these meetings with the Indians?—A. Well, sir, it was to make peace with the Indians and remove them off to some distant reservation, to keep them from spilling more blood.

Q. To negotiate terms of peace?—A. Yes, sir; and put them on a piece of land where they could treat them well.

All of the above questions and answers of this witness were duly interpreted to the prisoners by the interpreters.

TOBY, Riddle's wife, an Indian, called for the prosecution, being duly sworn, testified as follows:

Question by the judge-advocate. What is your name; is your name Toby?—A. Yes.

Q. Are you the wife of Mr. Riddle here?—A. Yes, sir.

Q. Were you at the meeting of the peace commissioners with Captain Jack and the others, on the day of the death of General Canby and the others?—A. Yes.

Q. What Indians were there?—A. Captain Jack, Schonchis, (Ellen's man, who is dead,) Black Jim, Hooka Jim, Schacknasty Jim, Boston Charley, and Bogus Charley.

Q. Did you go down there to that meeting with your husband?—A. Yes, sir.

Q. Did you stay there after he went away?—A. Yes, sir.

Q. What did you see happen there; what did Captain Jack do?—A. Captain Jack shot General Canby. The first time Schonchis missed Mr. Meacham.

Q. Did you see Schonchis fire at Mr. Meacham?—A. Yes; and he missed him the first time.

Q. And then what happened?—A. Hooka Jim was running after Mr. Dyer, and shooting at him.

Q. Did Schonchis fire twice?—A. I don't know exactly how many times he shot; he shot several times, though.

Q. At Mr. Meacham?—A. Yes, sir.

Q. Did you see Dr. Thomas shot?—A. Yes.

Q. Who shot him?—A. Boston Charley.

Q. Who fired first?—A. Captain Jack.

Q. Then when did the firing begin afterward; immediately or some time after?—A. They all commenced firing right after that, then.

Q. Did any other men join the party?—A. Yes.

Q. When did they join the party of Indians. How many of them joined the party?—A. I saw three men come up.

Q. Do you see any of them here?—A. Brancho was one; Lolocksalt, or Schlolox.

Q. Did anybody strike, or wound, or hurt you?—A. Yes, sir.

Q. Who was it?—A. Schlolox.

Q. What did he do to you?—A. He hit me across the back.

Q. What with?—A. A gun.

Q. Did you fall off your horse, or sit on your horse?—A. I was on the ground.

Q. Did he knock you down?—A. Yes.

Q. Did you see your husband when he ran away?—A. Yes.

Q. Did anybody fire at him?—Yes; I seen three men after him.

Q. Can you say who those three men were?—A. Yes; Brancho, Shacknasty Jim, and Ellen's man—he is dead.

Q. The other men who came up, what did they come up for?—A. I didn't see them until they got right up in there.

Q. Did they have anything in their hands?—A. They were packing guns.

Q. How many guns did each have?—A. I think they had three apiece.

Q. Did Captain Jack do or say anything before he began to fire?—A. Captain Jack, when he got ready, said "atuck."

Q. What does that mean?—A. "We are all ready."

Q. Did he get up from his place, or sit where he was when he began to fire?—A. He got up and went out a little piece from there, and then came back.

Q. Where were you when he fired?—A. I was sitting or laying down, rather pretty close, sort of between Meacham and Riddle.

Q. Did you see a pistol in Captain Jack's hands?—A. Yes, sir.

Q. Did you see him fire it?—A. Yes, sir.

Q. And did you see a pistol in Schonchis's hand?—A. Yes.

Q. Did you see him fire that?—A. Yes, sir.

Q. Did you think they were going to kill the commissioners that day?—A. Yes.

Q. What made you think so?—A. There was one of the other Indians told me so.

Q. Who told you?—A. William; Whim they call him.

Q. How long before the meeting did Whim tell you this?—A. It was about eight or ten days.

Q. What did Whim say to you?—A. He said not to come back any more; to tell the peace commissioners not to meet the Indians any more in counsel; that they were going to kill them.

Q. Did you tell General Canby not to go?—A. I did not tell General Canby; I told Meacham and Thomas.

Q. Did Mr. Meacham believe you?—A. Yes, sir.

Q. Did he say he believed you?—A. Yes.

Q. Did this Schlolox only strike you once?—A. Only once.

Q. Why didn't he strike you more than once?—A. Captain Jack and another Indian told him to let me alone; Black Jim there, and Jack.

Q. They told Schlolox to let you alone?—A. Yes, sir.

Q. Was he about to strike you again?—A. Yes; he was talking to me and trying to get the horse.

Q. Did you go with your husband the day before the meeting into Captain Jack's camp?—A. Yes, sir.

Q. Did you carry a message, or what did you go for?—A. I and he went in and took in a message from the peace commissioners; a written message.

Q. To whom?—A. To Captain Jack.

Q. What did Captain Jack say; did you hear him?—A. Yes.

Q. What did he say?—A. Jack said he was tired, and he didn't understand no papers. He didn't talk with any papers.

Q. What did Captain Jack say about a meeting; about the terms of a meeting?—A. He said that the old men made it up with him to have a meeting; at this side of the place Riddle spoke of.

Q. How many men were to go there?—A. Five men were to go there.

Q. Did he say anything about pistols, guns, or weapons?—A. He said he would not take any, and did not want the peace commissioners to take any.

Q. Did you go down from the peace commissioners' tent to the peace tent the day of the meeting and the murder?—A. Yes.

Q. Who did you go with?—A. I went along with Riddle, Dyer, and Mr. Meacham.

Q. How near to General Canby was Captain Jack when he fired?—A. He was right close to him.

Q. As near as you to me?—A. Yes, sir; (about 5 feet.)

Q. Was there a fire there burning?—A. There was a little fire there.

Q. How did they sit in reference to the fire. Did they sit away from or around it?—A. The fire had all gone out pretty nigh, and they were sitting pretty nigh the fire, most of them.

Q. How did Captain Jack fire; across the fire or over it, or sideways? A. It was out one side of the fire; General Canby was sitting one side of the fire, and Captain Jack walked around.

Q. Where did these two men, Sloluck and Brancho, come from when they came?—A. They came up from behind a kind of ridge of rocks about one hundred yards or such a matter from where the peace tent was.

Q. Had they been hiding behind there ?—A. Yes; I guess they had been hid there.

Q. Did you see them at first when you went to the meeting ?—A. No; I didn't see them.

Q. Where did you go after the deaths; after the firing ?—A. I went back to the camp then.

Q. You walked back ?—A. Yes, sir; I was leading the horse.

Q. What became of Captain Jack and the rest of the Indians ?—A. They all went back to Captain Jack's stronghold.

Q. Did they offer to do you any more harm ?—A. No; they didn't offer to touch me any more.

Q. What was done with the bodies of Dr. Thomas and General Canby ?—A. They stripped their clothes off of them.

Q. Did you see them do that ?—A. I seen them strip Dr. Thomas. I saw Steamboat Frank taking Dr. Thomas's coat. Steamboat Frank was one of the three that came up.

Q. Who were the three men that came up from behind the rocks ?—A. Steamboat Frank, Sloluck, and Brancho. There were more back there, but I didn't see them. I only know from what the Indians say.

The above questions and answers were duly interpreted to the prisoners by the sworn interpreter—Riddle.

The judge-advocate then asked the prisoners severally if they desired to cross examine the witness, to which they replied in the negative.

The commission had no question to put to the witness.

L. S. DYER, a citizen, called for the prosecution, being duly sworn, testified as follows :

Question by the judge-advocate: State your name.—Answer. L S. Dyer.

Q. What is your business ?—A. I am a United States Indian agent.

Q. Of the Klamath agency ?—A. Yes, sir.

Q. Does that include the Modocs ?—A. Yes, sir.

Q. Do you recognize the prisoners at the bar ?—A. I do.

Q. Do you recognize them all ?—A. No, sir.

Q. Who is that one with a handkerchief on his head ?—Captain Jack.

Q. Who is the next one this way ?—A. John Schonchis.

Q. And this one ?—A. Boston; sometimes called Boston Charley.

Q. You know them to be Modocs ?—A. That is what I understand them to be ; yes, sir.

Q. Did you occupy the position of peace commissioner ?—A. I did.

Q. In negotiation with the Modoc band ?—A. Yes, sir.

Q. By what appointment did you hold the position ?—A. I have never received a commission. I received a telegram from Thomas Benton Odeneal, informing me that I was appointed by, I won't say whether the Secretary of the Interior or of Indian Affairs.

Q. Were you appointed by some official in Washington ?—A. Yes. That telegram is lost.

Q. You never received a written commission ?—A. No, sir. I received a telegraphic dispatch from Superintendent Odeneal stating that I was appointed on the commission to treat with the Modocs, and requesting me to report the same immediately to headquarters.

Q. Were you recognized as such by the other commissioners ?—A. I was.

Q. What other reasons, if any, have you for supposing that that telegram was correct; have you been recognized as such in any other way?
—A. Yes, sir.

Q. Please state it.—A. At the time after the massacre I telegraphed to the Commissioner of Indian Affairs, stating the circumstances of the massacre, &c., signing myself as commissioner, and I received an answer as commissioner from the Commissioner of Indian Affairs.

Q. Can you tell whether Dr. Thomas received a written commission or simply a telegraphic notice?—A. He received a telegraphic appointment; no commission.

Q. Was that true of Mr. Meacham?—A. I cannot say as to that.

Q. You were recognized as a peace commissioner officially by telegraphic messages?—A. I cannot say as to Dr. Thomas. I was myself.

Q. And Mr. Meacham?—A. Mr. Meacham I know was recognized such.

Q. Did you enter upon any negotiations of peace with the Modoc band?—A. We did.

Q. With their representatives?—A. Yes.

Q. Whom or what did you represent at such negotiations?—A. We represented the United States; that is my understanding of the matter.

Q. When was the last meeting with the Modoc tribe?—A. On the 11th of April, 1873.

Q. Did they apply for a meeting or had an application for one been made by the commissioner? State the facts in regard to that.—A. This last meeting?

Q. Commencing from your connection with the peace commissioners; soon after or about the time General Gillem moved up there?—A. We sought an interview with the commission.

Q. How long before the 11th of April?—A. I cannot give the dates. Something more than a week, I think; perhaps ten days. That is according to my memory. I have not the statistics at all, and I have not the dates at all. It was a day or two after General Gillem moved over to the lava-beds.

Q. Was that the first meeting you had with them?—A. That was the first meeting we had with them. Well, we had seen some of them before. It was the first meeting we had with what we considered the leaders of the Modoc band.

Q. Did you have a meeting of the whole of the commissioners with Captain Jack soon after General Gillem moved over?—A. Yes. Boston and some others had been over to the camp at Van Bremer's before that, some time about the last of March.

Q. At that time, on the 11th, who were the Indians that you met?—A. I cannot give them all. The first meeting after arriving at Tule Lake we met Captain Jack, Schonchis, Scarfaced Charley, and Boston, and there were several others. I have forgotten them, some of them.

Q. After that, did you receive any notice of danger or caution?—A. We did.

Q. State it, if you please.—A. Mr. Riddle told us—told me; I think the rest of the commission——

Q. (Interrupting.) Who is Riddle?—A. He was acting as interpreter. Riddle said that his wife, Toby, as she was called, said that she was warned by an Indian.

Q. Did Toby herself warn you?—A. I think I did not hear Toby say so.

Q. The interpreter cautioned you, then, at any rate?—A. Yes, sir.

Q. You must not testify to what anybody else said, unless they said it to you. You say you did receive caution?—A. Yes, we received caution.

Q. What was the character of the caution; please state that?—A. That the Modocs meant to kill us.

Q. Was that after your first meeting?—A. Yes, sir.

Q. Before the meeting of the 11th of April?—A. Yes, sir.

Q. What was the result of that first meeting; did it result in some agreement or nothing?—A. There was very little. A portion of the commission thought that the prospect was favorable. Some little concessions were made on the part of the Modocs, and a portion of the commission thought that the prospect was rather favorable for further concession.

Q. Then was there any request made for another meeting by either party shortly after the first one?—A. Yes, sir; an arrangement was made.

Q. Who made the request, the commissioners or the Modocs?—A. The commission applied for a meeting, I think.

Q. Who were members of that commission?—A. Mr. Meacham, as chairman, Dr. Thomas, and myself and Judge Roseborough.

Q. Did that meeting take place?—A. A meeting took place.

Q. Did you go to it?—A. No, sir; the next meeting did not take place, I think. I may be in error as to dates, but a meeting was sought, and a place appointed by the Modocs for the meeting that they did not deem it advisable to go to.

Q. That was another meeting; that was still a third meeting. How many meetings did you have with the Modocs?—A. We had three.

Q. Who suggested the third meeting, then?—A. There was a meeting suggested in which but one of the commissioners was requested to be present, Mr. Meacham, and Judge Rosborough, two; no others. That meeting was requested by the Modocs.

Q. Did that meeting take place?—A. That meeting took place; yes, sir.

Q. Did you go?—A. As I understood it we were requesting a meeting, and they sent word that they would like to meet the commission, or would like to meet Judge Rosborough and Fairchilds; and would like to have Mr. Meacham go to hear what they had to say, but they didn't wish him to talk. I wish to correct myself. We were negotiating for meetings with those Indians, and at one time—whether it was after the second meeting, or after and next to the first meeting—a place was appointed by them where they would meet us, and we did not deem it advisable to go there.

Q. What place was that?—A. I really cannot tell whether that was after the first meeting or after the second meeting.

Q. You had three meetings?—A. A portion of the commission had three meetings.

Q. Which was the meeting at which General Canby and Dr. Thomas were killed?—A. That was the third meeting; at the second meeting there were only two of the commissioners present.

Q. Then I understand you to say the Indians proposed a place which you thought unadvisable to go to?—A. I cannot say whether it was before this second meeting or afterward. I have not the dates clearly in my mind.

Q. Where was the place that they proposed?—A. It was under a bluff of rocks.

Q. Nearer the lava-beds, or farther from them?—A. It was nearer the lava-beds than we had ever met them, perhaps half or two-thirds of the way from the camp to the lava-beds, under a large bluff of rocks.

Q. Why did you think it was unadvisable to go there?—A. I thought it was unadvisable because we had been warned of danger, and we thought that that indicated that they did mean treachery; taking us away off there where we would be entirely in their hands, and where as many of them could gather together as chose.

Q. Who warned you?—A. Riddle warned us that there was danger. He warned me.

Q. What were the terms proposed for that meeting; how many men were to go; and were they to go armed or unarmed? State the facts in a detailed form, if you can. What was the proposition and the terms made for this third meeting that you thought it unadvisable to go to? Were the Modocs to be armed or unarmed?—A. Armed; five men. I think they agreed to meet us equal numbers—five of us and five of them. I would not state this as positive; but if I recollect aright we were five of us to meet five of them armed.

Q. You think the Modocs proposed to meet you armed?—A. Yes, sir.

Q. Are you sure of that?—A. I think I am sure of it.

Q. Who brought these terms over to you? How did you become acquainted with those terms?—A. I will not be sure; I think it was through Boston. I am not sure of it. These things I have not kept in my mind at all.

Q. Now, let us go the meeting on the 11th of April, when General Canby was killed. Let us get the facts of that. What arrangements were entered into for a meeting? Who undertook them?—A. Boston.

Q. And anybody else? Go on.—A. Boston came in that morning to the camp early, and told us that Captain Jack would meet us at the tent.

Q. Did he state the terms?—A. Unarmed.

Q. How many on each side?—A. That they would meet five of us and five of them. I am not sure whether they said five beside Boston and Charley, who were then in camp. I cannot say positively whether there was to be five besides them or five including Boston and Bogus Charley, who were in camp.

Q. What was the purpose of this meeting?—A. It was to come to some conclusion; that was the understanding.

Q. A conclusion on what subject?—A. With regard to what the Modocs would do, or were willing to do, on the subject of peace.

Q. Did you receive any warning on that day that there was any danger?—A. No, sir.

Q. Do you know whether some of the other commissioners received any warning?—A. I don't know that they did; that is, any positive warning that there was danger particularly on that day.

Q. I don't ask particularly on that day. Did you receive any notice on that day that there might be danger on that day?—A. Yes, sir. I think it might be considered as a warning there might be danger on that day.

Q. Before deciding to go on that meeting did you go anywhere, and if so, where?—A. Not before deciding to go.

Q. Before going did you go anywhere else?—A. Before going, Mr. Riddle, our interpreter, requested us to go to General Gillem's tent with him.

Q. For what purpose? State in full.—A. After he got there he told General Gillem in our hearing—a portion of us; General Canby did not go into the tent—he told us that he wished General Gillem; the idea was this, that he wished General Gillem to understand that he had warned us that there was danger; that he didn't know that there was danger that day; but he was satisfied that there was danger, and he wished General Gillem to understand that he had warned us of that danger so that he would stand clear of all trouble; he stated that he thought there was danger, but didn't know whether there was danger that day or not; but he wished it understood that he had warned us that there was danger, and it might be that day.

Q. Now, Mr. Dyer, who started first, or did you all go together down to this meeting from General Gillem's tent?—A. Dr. Thomas and General Canby started ahead, and Mr. Meacham, myself, and the interpreters followed.

Q. How far apart?—A. I think they had got perhaps one hundred and fifty yards.

Q. Was Mr. Meacham inclined to be reluctant about going, or disposed to doubt the truth of the warnings?—A. Reluctant.

Q. Were you also reluctant?—A. Yes.

Q. Why, then, did you two go?—A. I can't answer for Mr. Meacham.

Q. For yourself.—A. I thought that if I didn't go, and there was trouble, I would be blamed, perhaps considered a coward, and I had rather take the chances with the rest of them.

Q. When you got to the peace tent, whom did you find there?—A. We found Captain Jack, Schonchis, Hooker Jim, Black Jim; Boston and Bogus went with us; and there were two others. I may be mistaken in their names, but if I recollect aright the other two were Ellen's man and Shacknasty Jim.

Q. How many did you expect to find?—A. I expected to find five.

Q. How many were there?—A. Eight in all.

Q. What occurred then?—A. We talked, shook hands all around.

Q. And smoked?—A. I don't remember.

Q. Where did you take your seat?—A. At first very near Captain Jack and Schonchis, a little one side and behind.

Q. Could you see anything peculiar in their appearance, anything suggesting danger?—A. I saw they both had pistols under their coats; their coats stuck out, and I supposed they had revolvers.

Q. The agreement was they should go unarmed?—A. Yes.

Q. And you saw what you took to be revolvers under their coats?—A. Yes.

Q. And the same appearance in the other men?—A. I didn't look at the others particularly; I didn't determine that.

Q. How long did you have this conversation?—A. I would like to state that I changed position after we had talked a few moments. A gentleman, Mr. Clark, made his appearance—following us up, in fact, quite a distance back—and the Indians seemed dissatisfied that there should be any other person near or in sight; and by Mr. Meacham's request I went back and requested him to go back to camp, and then I returned and stopped a little back from where I was before, and did not go into the circle. I sat a little reclined on the ground, a little back, holding my horse.

Q. Did Captain Jack keep his position all the time?—A. Until we had talked perhaps an hour, and then he got up and said he must go back and (in a vulgar way) attend to the calls of nature.

Q. And then did he go back?—A. Yes.

Q. And what then? Give a detail of the affair; a picture of it?—A. Schonchis was talking. It was while Schonchis was talking that Jack went back. He returned in a few moments, and as he approached the circle, a step perhaps or two, a very few feet from where he had been sitting, he snapped a cap; snapped his pistol.

Q. You saw the pistol ?—A. I did. He said about the same time, "Attuck," or words similar; meaning, I understand, "all ready" or "now;" something of that nature.

Q. He snapped a cap, and what else happened ?—A. I looked up the instant I heard the cap snap, and saw he was aiming his pistol at General Canby; I think he was. When I first threw my head up he had not taken it, the pistol, from snapping the cap; then he cocked it immediately.

Q. Did you see General Canby at this time ?—A. No, sir. It was in General Canby's direction I had seen him.

Q. But you did not look at him at that moment ?—A. I did not.

Q. Did you see Jack aim at him ?—A. Yes, at where he was sitting, as near as I could judge. Then I sprang up to run, and at just about the instant I sprang his pistol went off.

Q. What else did you see, if anything ?—A. I saw nothing more of what they were doing until I had ran about 150 yards.

Q. Were you chased ?—A. Yes.

Q. Did you stop and look around ?—A. Yes, I heard some one after me, and had heard shooting and balls whistling about me, and I supposed it was one of the Indians, and I turned about and faced him.

Q. Could you see who it was ?—A. Yes, Hooka Jim.

Q. How soon after the cap snapping did the pistol go off ?—A. In a very few seconds, perhaps two or three. He cocked his pistol and fired again.

Q. Was there more firing after that ?—A. Yes, a good deal.

Q. What interval occurred between the firing at General Canby and the other firing which followed ?—A. It was very near together.

Q. Do you mean almost simultaneous ?—A. Yes, almost, perhaps a few seconds' interval.

Q. This peace commission interview on the 11th April, did it take place during a cessation of arms ?—A. Yes.

Q. Was there no fighting at that time ?—A. No.

Q. Have you ever seen any fighting since you have been a peace commissioner ?—A. I had not before this.

Q. Have you any grounds of learning by whom this Modoc band was commanded in the lava-beds ?—A. By Captain Jack.

Q. Did this party represent the Modoc band ?—Yes, they were the leaders, perhaps not all of them, but a portion of the leaders.

Q. General Canby, yourself, Mr. Meacham, and Dr. Thomas represented what ?—A. The United States.

Q. Were you injured on the 11th April ? Did you receive any personal injury ?—A. No.

Q. Received no wounds ?—A. None.

Q. Have you any doubt the intent was to wound and kill you ?—A. I judge so.

Q. You so judge from the pistol-balls flying about you ?—A. Yes.

Q. Do you know Mr. Odeneal ?—A. Yes.

Q. What position does he hold here ?—A. Up to June 30, 1873, he was superintendent of Indian affairs for Oregon.

Q. Who holds the position now ?—A. I don't know. I understand the superintendency for Oregon has been done away with.

Q. Have you ever seen a treaty between the United States and the Modocs ?—A. I have.

Q. Have you it in your posssssion ?—A. I have.

Q. Have you read it ?—A. Yes.

Q. What is the provision in reference to the Modocs and the reservation set apart for them ?—A. The provision is—I cannot give all the particulars—that they shall reside on the reservation.

Q. Had this party of Modocs headed by Captain Jack adhered to that agreement?—A. According to my understanding they had not, this party.

Q. How long have they been in disobedience?—A. A portion ever since the treaty was framed, as I understand it; they have been brought upon the reservation and ran away.

Q. Who was superintendent before Odeneal?—A. A. B. Meacham.

Q. Do you know of your own knowledge whether Mr. Meacham had ever tried to return them to the reservation ?—A. Yes, he had.

Q. Often, more than once ?—A. Once he brought them back.

Q. What followed on that ?—A. They remained through the winter, until they could get a good living off the reservation, and then ran away.

Q. Did you see the body of General Canby dead ?—Yes.

Q. Recognzie it ?—A. Yes.

Q. And of Dr. Thomas ?—A. Yes.

Q. And knew it also ?—A. Yes.

Q. What position did General Canby occupy toward the peace commission. I mean was he one of them ?—A. The commission did not understand it exactly so. They did not understand that he was a member of the commission, but that he had a supervision of the action of the commission, and they were expected always to act by his advice and were never contrary to it—in accord with him by his advice and in conjunction with him.

The prisoners, on being severally asked if they desired to put any questions to the witness, answered in the negative.

Question by commission. After you were warned of the danger in meeting those leading men of the Modocs, was it your sense of duty as a commissioner that took you there, or fear that you would be known in the world as a coward if you had not gone ?—A. Both. I feared that if I didn't go, or if Meacham and I didn't go, the commission would be a failure, and there might be a failure through our not going ; that was one reason. Another way was that we would also be branded as coward, and it would be generally understood that the commission failed because of our cowardice ; it was both of these.

Question by commission. I understood you to say that Superintendent Meacham got these Modocs back into the reservation once or twice before ?—A. Once before.

Question by commission. With or without the assistance of the military ?—A. He had a few soldiers. I only know this from the records and reports in the office.

The foregoing questions and answers were all duly interpreted to the prisoners.

The commission thereupon adjourned to meet on Monday next, the 7th instant, at 10 a. m.

H. P. CURTIS,
Judge-Advocate of Commission.

154   MODOC WAR.

THIRD DAY.

FORT KLAMATH, OREGON,
July 7, 1873.

The commission met pursuant to adjournment.

Present, all the members named in the order, the judge-advocate, and the prisoners.

The proceedings of the previous session were read and approved.

SHACKNASTY JIM, a Modoc Indian, a witness for the prosecution, having been first cautioned by the judge-advocate of the punishment of false swearing, was then duly sworn.

Question by judge-advocate. What is your name?—Answer. Shack-nasty Jim.

Q. Do you remember when General Canby was killed?—A. Yes; I know.

Q. Were you present?—A. Yes.

Q. Did you know that he and the commissioners were to be killed?—A. Yes.

Q. How did you know it?—A. They had a talk at night.

Q. When was this talk? How long before?—A. The evening before.

Q. Who talked?—A. Most of the Indians; the two chiefs were talking.

Q. What two chiefs?—A. Captain Jack and Schonchis.

Q. Did you hear them state they meant to kill them?—A. I didn't hear them say they were going to kill them.

Q. What did you hear them say?—A. I heard them talking about killing the commissioners; that is all I heard them say. I didn't hear them say who was going to do it.

Q. How long before the meeting of the peace commissioners when General Canby was killed was this talk?—A. I almost forget. I don't want to lie. I have forgotten how many days it was.

Q. What Indians were at that meeting of April 11, when General Canby was shot?—A. Schonchis, Captain Jack, Ellen's man, (dead.) I was there and Black Jim, Boston, Bogus Charley, and Hooker Jim; there were eight.

Q. Did any come up afterward?—A. After they began shooting, Barncho and Slolluck and Steamboat Frank and Scar-faced Charley. Steamboat and Scar-face were still in behind the other two after the firing had commenced, or was about over.

Q. Did Slolluck and Barncho have anything in their hands?—A. Packing guns.

Q. Did you see anything done?—A. Yes; I saw Captain Jack shoot General Canby.

Q. Did any one else shoot General Canby?—A. Ellen's man, after Jack had shot him, shot him once.

Q. Did Schonchis take any part?—A. He shot at Meacham.

Q. What did Barncho do, if anything?—A. He ran Riddle, and was shooting after him.

Q. What did you do yourself?—A. I was running after Riddle.

Q. Who told you there was to be killing?—A. I heard them talking about it.

The judge-advocate then asked each of the prisoners if he wished to examine the witness, to which they severally replied in the negative.

Question by commissioner. I would like to inquire what Boston did at the time of the firing?—A. He shot Dr. Thomas.

Question by commissioner. And Black Jim ?—A. He was after Meacham.

Q. Did you see Black Jim discharge his pistol or gun ?—A. Yes; I saw him fire.

Q. Did you see Slolluck do anything?—A. I saw him close to the woman Toby. But the tent was sort between them and me, and I didn't see what they done. But he was there among them.

Question by judge-advocate. Did you hear Captain Jack say anything before the firing?—A. I was off a good ways from him, and didn't hear him say anything. I was laying down on my blanket when the firing commenced.

STEAMBOAT FRANK, a Modoc witness for the prosecution, duly sworn, being duly warned against the consequences of perjury.

Question by judge-advocate. What is your name?—Answer. I am called Steamboat Frank.

Q. Were you present at the death of General Canby ?—A. Yes.

Q. How did you get there ?—A. I was about as far as from here to the end of the stables (about four hundred yards) when the firing commenced.

Q. Whom, if any one, were you with there?—A. With Scar-faced Charley.

Q. Who else ?—A. No one.

Q. Did you see Barncho ?—A. I seen him before they started in there.

Q. Any one else ?—A. I seen another, an old man, who has no English name.

Q. Did you have anything with you when you came up ?—A. I had my gun.

Q. Did you know that the death was determined on ?—A. I knew they were going to kill the peace commissioners.

Q. How did you know it ?—A. I heard the Indians talking about the killing of General Canby.

Q. What Indians ?—A. Captain Jack and Schonchis talking about it.

Q. Who proposed it ?—A. Captain Jack.

Q. When did you hear this ?—A. The day before and that evening I heard them.

Q. How did you come behind the rocks ?—A. I was laying there and was not doing anything.

Q. Why did you go there?—A. I wanted to see if they would kill General Canby.

Q. Did you go of your own accord ?—A. Captain Jack told me to come there.

Q. Did you shoot anybody ?—A. No, sir.

The prisoners being severally asked if they desired to examine this witness, answered in the negative.

The commission had no questions to ask.

L. S. DYER re-examined by the judge-advocate.

Question. You stated yesterday you had the treaty of the United States with Modocs in your possession ?—Answer. Yes.

Q. Do you wish to correct your testimony ?—A. I do.

Q. In what ?—A. I wish to say that I have what I suppose to be a copy of that treaty. I supposed when giving my testimony before that it was the original, as it says on the article " original treaty," &c.

Q. Do you know it to be a correct copy?—A. On close examination I find it is not the original, but that I take it to be a copy. I don't know that it is a copy.

Q. You stated Saturday, at the last session, that by the treaty the commission had no right to return the Modocs to their reservation?—A. I certainly do.

Q. Can you testify as positively to that now, finding the treaty to be' as you say, as you could then?—A. If this is a correct copy of the treaty I can, otherwise I can not.

Question by commission. By whom is your copy of the treaty authenticated as a true copy?—A. It is not authenticated as a copy.

The judge-advocate stated to the commission that at the last session he had alluded to the treaty in question inadvertently and irrelevantly; but having done so, he had intended to attach to the record a verified copy of it, but finding that Mr. Dyer has no verified copy, and that it is not the original which he has, it was impossible for him to do so. He regards it, however, as unnecessary, as the whole subject is irrelevant to the issue before the commission.

Question by judge-advocate. Do you know Rev. Dr. Thomas's Christian name?—A. I have seen it given as Eleazen.

Q. You are a citizen of the United States?—A. Yes.

The foregoing having been fully interpreted to the prisoners,

The judge-advocate now called BOGUS CHARLEY as witness for the prosecution, who, being first cautioned of the consequence of perjury, was duly sworn, and testified as follows:

Question by judge-advocate. What is your name as commonly called?—Answer. Bogus Charley.

Q. Were you present at the death of General Canby?—A. Yes.

Q. Did you know he and the others were to be killed?—A. I didn't know it at that time.

Q. What do you mean by that?—A. I didn't know they were going to kill them.

Q. Do you mean on that particular day?—A. I had heard them talk a little, but never heard them say but very little about it.

Q. Whom do you mean by them?—A. I heard Captain Jack talking a little about it, and Schonchis.

Q. Did anybody else tell you?—A. Whim, or William, told me.

Q. What did he tell you?—A. He told me they were going to kill them men—the commissioners—while they were talking good talk.

The judge-advocate then asked each prisoner, successively, if he desired to cross-examine the witness; to which they severally answered in the negative.

Question by judge-advocate. Have you had any quarrel with Jack?—A. I had a quarrel with Captain Jack at the Dry Lake, south of the lava-bed.

Q. Do you now like or dislike him?—A. I don't like him very well now.

The commission had no questions to offer.

HOCKER JIM, a Modoc, a witness for the prosecution; and first cautioned of the consequence and punishment for perjury, duly sworn.

Question. What is your English name?—Answer. Hocker Jim.

Q. Were you present when General Canby was killed?—A. I was.

Q. Did you know he and the commissioners were to be killed?—A. I did.

Q. Are you now a friend to Captain Jack?—A. I have been a friend of Captain Jack, but I don't know what he got mad at me for.

Q. Have you ever had a quarrel or fight with him?—A. I had a quarrel and a little fight with him over to Dry Lake, beyond the lava-bed.

Q. How did you know the commissioners were going to be killed?—A. Captain Jack and Schonchis—I heard them talking about it.

Q. Where were they when you heard them?—A. At Captain Jack's house.

Question by commission. What part were you detailed to take in it, if any, in murdering the commissioners?—A. I ran Dyer and shot at him.

Question by commission. Had you agreed to kill one of the parties before the attack?—A. I said I would kill one if I could.

Question by judge-advocate. Do you like Captain Jack now or dislike him?—A. I don't like him very well now.

The judge-advocate then asked each one of the prisoners, successively, if they desired to cross-examine this witness, to which they replied in the negative.

WILLIAM, (WHIM,) Modoc, called for the prosecution, and warned against the penalties of perjury, was then duly sworn.

Question by judge-advocate. What is your name?—Answer. Whim, or William.

Q. Were you with the Modoc Indians in the lava-bed?—A. Yes.

Q. Do you remember when General Canby was killed?—A. Yes, I know that they went to kill him.

Q. Did you know that he was going to be killed?—A. Yes, I knew they were going to kill him.

Q. Did you know they were going to kill the peace commissioners?—A. Yes.

Q. Were you at the killing?—A. No, I didn't go.

Q. How did you know they were going to kill them?—A. I heard Jack and Schonchis talking about it.

Q. Any one else?—A. That is all that I heard say anything about it.

Q. How long was this before the killing?—A. I don't know exactly, but it was eight or ten days.

Q. Did you speak to anybody about it?—A. Yes, I told about it.

Q. Whom?—A. I told this woman here, (Toby Riddle's wife.)

Q. What did you tell her?—A. I told her to tell the peace commissioners not to come, that I did not want to see them killed.

The judge-advocate then asked each prisoner, successively, if he desired to cross examine this witness; each answered in the negative.

The commission desired to put no questions.

A. B. MEACHAM, citizen, called for the prosecution, duly sworn, testified as follows:

Question by judge-advocate. What is your name?—Answer. Alfred B. Meacham.

Q. Are you a citizen of the United States?—A. I am.

Q. What position did you hold in connection with the late war with the Modocs?—A. I was appointed by Secretary Delano as chairman of the peace commissioners, as special commissioner.

Q. At the time of the event now in course of investigation, who were your associates, if any?—A. Dr. Eleazer Thomas, of Petaluma, Cal., and Leroy S. Dyer, agent at Klamath, were the only associates present who were members of the commission.

Q. What position did General Canby hold?—A. As an adviser and counselor.

Q. Was General Canby in receipt of instructions from Washington, in reference to this matter,·to your knowledge?—A. Yes.

Q. And you were directed to consult with him?—A. Yes, to consult and advise, and, as far as possible, to co-operate with him.

Q. Do you recognize any of the prisoners?—A. I do.

Q. Whom of them?—A. Captain Jack, Schonchis, John, and Boston. I am not sure of the names of the others. I recognize the faces of two others there, but am not sure of their names.

Q. Was Dr. Thomas a citizen of the United States?—A. He was.

Q. Whom or what did you represent, the commissioners I mean, in your negotiations with the Modocs?—A. I understood that we were representing the Interior Department of the Government; representing the Government of the United States through the Interior Department.

Q. Did you have meetings with the Indians in April last?—A. Yes.

Q. On what days?—A. We had two in April; the first was on the 3d, if my memory is correct; the second official meeting was on the 11th.

Q. Was that the last?—A. That was the last.

Q. When you met these prisoners on the 11th April did you meet them as representatives of the Modoc band?—A. Yes.

Q. What was the purpose of that meeting?—A. To arrange the details of their surrender,.to a peaceful end, as I understood.

Q. To bring the matter to a peaceful end?—A. Yes.

Q. Now will you state the circumstances which preceded and led to the meeting of the 11th April?—A. Do you desire me to state the arrangement for the meeting and its history, or simply the meeting itself?

Q. The history of the arrangements for the meeting, and all the events connected with the homicide, not going back too far.—A. After the first meeting of the 3d April there seemed to have been some difficulty about securing a second meeting. On the 6th April I met all of these men, and one or two others, I think, in an unofficial way, at the council-tent, but made no positive arrangements for a subsequent meeting; failed to do it. On perhaps the 7th, Mrs. Riddle, who was employed as interpreter, was sent as messenger to Jack's camp to make an effort to secure a meeting, and came back saying that no meeting could be safely had, that assassination had been determined on, and she had been so notified. This fact she did not communicate to the board directly, though she did to me through her husband. I laid the fact before the board myself. On the 8th Boston Charley—Boston as he is commonly called—came into camp, as a messenger from Jack's camp, proposing a meeting.

Q. What were the terms of this proposed meeting?—A. He made four propositions; the first, to meet them near Jack's stronghold, to come five men, and armed if we chose, designating who the men should be, to consist of General Canby, General Gillem, Dr. Thomas, Mr. Dyer, and myself; if we elected so to do, to bring arms. The alternative was that they would then meet us next day at the council-tent. That was the first proposition.

Q. You said there were four propositions; you have stated two.—A.

I intended to state but one, but I have really stated two, but not regularly.

Q. Please go on.—A. That proposition, then, was refused. Then, as a further inducement, that if we would meet them on the first terms proposed, near Captain Jack's camp, that they would meet us the next day at the headquarters, General Gillem's camp. That was the second proposition.

Q. Were those terms accepted?—A. Neither one of those terms were accepted. Then Boston stated that Captain Jack said: "You meet us at the council-tent to-morrow, and next day we will meet you in the headquarters." That was the third proposition.

Q. Was any mention made about arms or numbers?—A. On the first two propositions we were to meet armed, if we chose. The proposition at the council-tent did not suggest that we should go armed.

Q. Did it suggest that you should come unarmed?—A. I don't think it did, sir; I have no recollection that it did.

Q. This was on the 7th, I think, you said?—A. I think it was the 7th.

Q. About that time?—A. Yes, sir. The fourth proposition was, that if we would meet them at the council-tent unarmed, that Captain Jack and his people would come into camp and bring all the goods he had and lay them down before the general. All of these propositions were rejected.

Q. What was the place designated in the first proposition? What was the place which Captain Jack finally designated as the place for meeting, near his stronghold?—A. Near his stronghold, and, if my memory is correct, it had reference to the place of the first meeting on the 3d of April.

Q. What was its character?—A. The first meeting took place in one of these large sink-holes. It is all rocky; a hole in the sunken rocks, which was deep enough to hold a small army almost. It was very rocky; a place that could be very easily surrounded.

Q. And this was the place he desired you to meet him?—A. That is my understanding. He desired us to meet at the same place we had the first meeting.

Q. You rejected these proposals?—A. These proposals were all rejected.

Q. Then what came next?—A. The proposition sent back by us that we would meet Captain Jack on equal terms at the council-tent, on even terms. My memory is not good enough to give you the whole force of the proposition. I know that that was the substance of it.

Q. What was the meaning of that?—A. The meaning of that was that we were always willing to meet and have a talk, but we wanted to go in a way that we would feel secure. We did not want them to have the advantage. Then Captain Jack wanted to bring an armed company of men with him, and that he would allow us to do the same thing; that we would agree to the same proposition. That is the substance of the message that was sent back by Boston in reply to Captain Jack's overtures for this meeting.

Q. What further occurred after these circumstances you have been detailing, these propositions being rejected?—A. I am wrong in my dates that I have given you, sir. I was trusting to my memory, and I find by memoranda I was not quite correct in the dates. That this meeting when the four propositions were made occurred on Sunday, I am very sure; and that on Monday Boston returned.

Q. What day was Sunday?—A. Sunday must have been the 6th.

Q. And on the 7th Boston returned?—A. And on the 7th Boston

returned and desired that Frank Riddle should go out and give Captain Jack advice. Frank Riddle was sent by the commission with instructions what to say to Captain Jack and his people. Captain Jack sent his reply by Riddle that he would not come to the tent to talk.

Q. Was that the advice that was given to Riddle to convey to him?—A. I believe I have the memoranda. My recollection is we instructed Riddle to say we were still willing to meet him at the tent on any terms that would be satisfactory.

Q. And did he refuse to come?—A. He refused to come to the tent; but still insisted he was willing to meet us near his camp. He was unwilling to meet us at the council-tent until the soldiers were all taken away, after which he would be willing to meet and talk with us at the council-tent about a new reservation. That he was unwilling to talk about any other place than Fairchild's ranch or Cottonwood Hot Creek, I believe it is called; he was unwilling to talk about any other place. That was the proposition. That was his reply to Riddle.

Q. Was this place which he first designated near the stronghold a dangerous place for the commissioners to meet him?—A. We considered it very dangerous then. We were unwilling to go on account of the danger. It was too far from the military camp. It was nearer Captain Jack's camp than ours, and a very rough portion of the lava-bed.

Q. Was it so that men might be concealed there?—A. It was.

Q. Was it a position that could be commanded?—A. It was a position that might be commanded, and men might be concealed to any number. That was our objection to meeting there.

Q. Then who made the next proposition, and what was it?—A. The next proposition again came from Captain Jack, through Boston. After Riddle's visit Boston again came and made a proposition.

Q. What are those papers you are looking at?—A. Memoranda taken by me at the time.

Q. Memoranda made by yourself?—A. They are, sir.

Q. Do you wish to refresh your memory by them?—A. I do, sir; to be sure I am right.

Q. What was the proposition from Captain Jack then?—A. To meet at the council-tent.

Q. In what way, armed or unarmed?—A. I am unable to state what that proposition was.

Q. What action did the commissioners take upon that?—A. This last proposal of which I am speaking was made by Boston, with the assurance that Captain Jack and five men were there waiting for us at the council-tent. We were informed that such was the fact, and that in addition to it some twenty or thirty men were behind them in the rocks. I don't know through what source this information came; only it was from the station on the hillside. We refused to go that day; that was Wednesday; it must have been the 9th. On Thursday Boston again came in with the message from Captain Jack, accompanied by Hooker Jim, William, and Dave. The propositions that were made that day I didn't hear; I have only the memoranda and information from Dr. Thomas. I don't know whether it is proper or not.

Q. We won't take that. Now state what occurred next.—A. During the day the propositions that were made by Boston, that is, on Thursday, were accepted by Dr. Thomas, and an agreement made to meet Captain Jack and five men, unarmed, at 11 o'clock; all parties unarmed at the council-tent on Friday. I knew this agreement to have been made by Dr. Thomas on the evening of the 10th, on my return from Boyle's camp that night.

Q. Did he give it to you officially ?—A. Yes, sir. When I started on the visit to Boyle's camp, I said to Dr. Thomas, if occasion requires my presence in any business, you will act in my capacity as chairman of the commission, and as acting chairman of the commission he made this arrangement, and so notified me.

Q. After that what followed ?—A. I protested against the meeting, but subsequently yielded to the opinions of General Canby and Dr. Thomas, Mr. Dyar and I dissenting. We yielded to their judgment, and we consented that the meeting should take place. Before starting, Mr. Riddle, our interpreter, asked an interview with the board, which was granted, at which time he remarked that he thought there was great danger in going, and that he wanted to be clear of the responsibility; that his wife and he had lived together for twelve years, and that she had never deceived him; that he believed those Indians meant treachery. This was made in the presence of General Gillem, Dr. Thomas, Mr. Dyar, and myself, General Canby being at the tent door, but not in hearing. After Mr. Riddle retired, General Canby expressed his doubts about danger. Dr. Thomas also said that he was still willing to go. The subject-matter of Mr. Riddle's communication was given to General Canby by myself before starting to the lava-bed. General Canby's opinion, or his reply, was pretty nearly in these words: " I think there is no danger; although I have no more confidence in these Indians than you have; I think them capable of it; but they dare not do it; it is not to their interest." With this assurance, and the confidence I had in General Canby, I gave a reluctant assent to the meeting on my part; and Mr. Dyar, as I then understood, did also. General Canby and Dr. Thomas started afoot and alone, going past the tent occupied by the peace commissioners. At the door of the tent Mrs. Riddle was holding my horse. She protested against the meeting; that there was danger, or something of that kind. Mr. Dyar had remarked, too, that he thought there was danger. I called to General Canby and Dr. Thomas, who had, perhaps, gone past the tent occupied by the commission one hundred yards. They waited until I approached them, and we had another conversation on the subject, General Canby saying to me, to allay my fears, that I was unduly cautious; that with the disposition of the troops, these Indians dare not do it, and he repeated to me again that he had no more confidence in them than I had; but that it could not be to their interest; that they did not dare to do it; that Colonel Mason was only a short distance from their stronghold, and before they could get back to their council-tent Colonel Mason's force could be put into the stronghold on to them; that he had had the road watched from the signal-station with a glass since daylight this morning—that was the morning of the 11th; that there was but five Indians there, and they were apparently unarmed; that I should allay my fears, for he had none under the circumstances, or pretty near to that effect.

Q. Do I understand you to say this meeting was brought about by a messenger from Captain Jack ?—A. From Captain Jack; arranged by Dr. Thomas, with the consent of General Canby, by a messenger sent by Captain Jack, Boston, who remained over-night in the camp. Dr. Thomas didn't believe there was danger; he told me so. He thought there could be no danger. General Canby's opinion seemed to be pretty nearly his: that he felt he was in the line of duty; that he was serving God, and that if God required his life he was ready; that he was going at all events. I made the proposition, if this meeting must take place, that we go armed, and that John Fairchilds be allowed to go along; that I was willing to go with John Fairchilds armed and I armed, if no one else was. Dr. Thomas strenuously opposed this, because it would be a breach of the compact. I insisted that I knew these people better than he did; that they would not keep their part of the campact; that they would be armed, and there would be more than five of them there. The doctor again replied, in a very religious way, that it was a matter belonging to God; that we would keep our part of the compact and trust to Him. I made one further proposition, I remember distinctly: that if, when we arrived on the ground, things looked dangerous, I would make them any promise in the world rather than that they should have my life or theirs. Dr. Thomas says, "I will be a party to no deception under any circumstances; this matter is in the hands of God." General Canby said, "I have dealt with Indians for thirty years, and I have never deceived an Indian, and I will not consent to it—to any promise that cannot be fulfilled." There was other conversation that I don't suppose is pertinent. I wanted that on record. I abandoned all idea of persuading or dissuading them from going, and I went again to the commission-tent, where Mr. Dyer was saddling his horse. John Fairchild was there also, and Mrs. Riddle was then holding my horse, and Mr. Riddle, I think, preparing my horse to ride, and Bogus Charley was there. I asked Fairchilds what he thought of the situation, and, without giving any definite answer, he said he would talk to Bogus Charley; that he could tell by his talk whether there was danger or not. He had the talk with Bogus Charley, and came back, and said he thought there could not be danger from the way Bogus talked; that Bogus assured him there was no danger.

Q. You then went to the peace-tent?—A. Yes, sir. There are one or two other points I wish to go on the record. After that talk with Bogus, Mr. Fairchilds and I had still another conversation, in which we agreed exactly; we still thought there was danger. I remarked to Mr. Dyer that I saw no reason why he was in honor bound to go; as chairman of this commission, my honor compelled me to go; that I was not willing to have Dr. Thomas and General Canby go alone. I remember Mr. Dyer's reply was, if I went he was going. I then gave what money I had to Mr. Fairchilds, and Mr. Dyer did the same, and we started, perhaps two hundred yards behind Dr. Thomas and General Canby; Mr. Dyer on horseback, Mrs. Riddle riding a horse, I was on horseback, Mr. Riddle was afoot, and Bogus Charley started with us, but I don't think he went, all of the way out, along with us; it is my impression that he did not. We went a longer route in going to the council-tent than General Canby and Dr. Thomas did, requiring several minutes more to make the journey. When we arrived at the council-tent, Boston had already arrived, and I think Bogus was ahead of us also, making seven Indians who were there present, visible, and they were all smoking; I think all smoking except Dr. Thomas, who never smoked; they were smoking the cigars which General Canby had carried out. There had been a little fire built fifteen or twenty feet off the council-tent, and on the side directly opposite from our camp, a sage-brush fire. General Canby and Dr. Thomas were standing nearest to the tent when we arrived, nearer than the Indians were; and around this little fire, which had nearly burned out, my recollection is, there were either stones there naturally, or there had been some stones placed around, making a kind of half-circle, or three-fourths of a circle. Before dismounting from my horse I had taken my overcoat off, laying it on the horn of the saddle in front of me. When I dismounted I hung my overcoat on the horn of the saddle, and dropped the rope of my horse on the ground, without tying him; reining him up with the bridle-rein, over the coat, holding it to the horn of the saddle. Mr. Dyer rode on to the east side of the fire before dismounting, my opinion is, and also Mrs. Riddle. When we got ready for the talk, we sat down around this fire; General Canby facing Schonchin John, those two being nearest the tent; Captain Jack sat next to Schonchin John, and there were other Indians next to Captain Jack, but I cannot say who now. I can only define positively the position of Captain Jack and Schonchin; that I sat next to General Canby, on his left; that Dr. Thomas sat down on the ground, not on a stone; and a little behind me, to my left again, Mrs. Riddle sat down or lay down on the ground, very close to Dr. Thomas, a little in front of him. Mr. Riddle, a portion of the time, was between Dr. Thomas and Mrs. Riddle; but, after we had been talking a few minutes, some of the Indians discovered a man approaching from the camp, and, at my request, Mr. Dyer mounted his horse, and rode out to the man, and sent him back again. On Mr. Dyer's return to the council, he dismounted from his horse on the side of the fire occupied by the Indians; to the right, properly speaking, of General Canby, and a little behind my horse. We had been talking perhaps fifteen minutes, when Hooker Jim went to my horse, calling him by name, and tied the rope either to a rock, or a little sage-brush grub; went to the saddle, and took my overcoat off and put it on, buttoned it up from bottom to top, and said he was Meacham, or that he would be Meacham. He turned to Bogus Charley, and asked him if he didn't look like old man Meacham.

Q. He said he was or he would be?—A. Yes, sir; but I cannot say which way. He said it one way or the other; that he was or would be Meacham. I am not very positive whether he said, "I am Meacham now," or "I will be Meacham." But one or the other. I know that he asked Bogus Charley if he looked like old Meacham, (as I think the Modocs called me.)

Q. Did he say it in English?—A. Yes; that act was, in my judgment, at that time a declaratory one, and sufficient evidence of what was coming. I sought to get a glance at General Canby's face, and I am very confident, although no words were passed, that General Canby understood the act and knew what it meant.

Q. That is not material. Please go on.—A. I think we talked fifteen or twenty minutes after that before any other demonstration was made of a hostile nature. Dr. Thomas had made a very religious and conciliatory speech to the Indians, General Canby a very friendly one, and Jack had finished talking, said he had talked all he wished to. Schonchin John was making a speech, which Riddle was interpreting. After Schonchin John had finished his speech, or made a statement or declaration, and while Riddle was interpreting it, off on our left and pretty near in range of the way we were sitting, two men that I did not recognize jumped up from ambush with one or more guns under each arm.

Q. Mr. Meacham, can you not tell the commission what General Canby said to the Indians?—A. Yes; I have a pretty good recollection of it. The substance I know exactly. After this demonstration of Hooker Jim's—the taking of the coat—fully appreciating the peril we were in, I asked General Canby if he had any remarks to make, partly for an opportunity to look him in the face, and partly to see whether he could say something that might avert the peril. General Canby rose to his feet to talk, and said, in substance, that when he was a very young officer in the Army he was detailed to remove two different tribes of Indians, one from Florida, and one from some other part of the southeast, to west of the Mississippi River; that at first they had not liked him very well, but after they got acquainted with him they liked him so well that they elected him chief among them. He then gave the name that each tribe had given him, one designating a tall man or chief, the other " the Indian's friend," giving the Indian word; that years after they were located in the new home he visited these people and found them prosperous and happy; that they came a long ways to meet and shake hands with him; that they greeted him as a friend and a brother; that he had no idea but what these Modocs would, some time or other, recognize him as a friend when they were located in a home; that his life, or the greater portion of it, had been spent in the United States Army, in the Indian service; that he had never deceived them, had always dealt fairly with them; that he came here at the request of the President of the United States; that the President had ordered the troops here, and that they could only be removed by the President's order; that they were only here for the purpose of seeing that this commission did their duty, and performed what they agreed to do. That these people (addressing them) should do what they had agreed to do, and that the citizens should not interfere. That unless the President ordered it, he, General Canby, " could not take the soldiers away." This is about a synopsis of the general's speech.

Dr. Thomas's speech, if you are willing to hear it, I would like to have on the record.

JUDGE-ADVOCATE. Certainly.—A. After General Canby had spoken I turned again to Doctor Thomas, who was a little behind me; and the Doctor in raising foward came upon his knees, and laid his right hand on my left shoulder, bringing him nearly even with me. In this position, on his knees, with his hand on my shoulder, he was so close to me, he said: " Toby, tell these people that I think the Great Spirit put it into the heart of the President to send us here. I have known General Canby for fourteen years; I have known Mr. Dyer for a few years, and Mr. Meacham for eighteen years; and I know their hearts, and I know they are all your friends; and I know my own heart and I believe that God sees us, what we do; that he wishes us all to be at peace; that no more blood should be shed." That is the substance; there were other little things, but they are immaterial.

I would now like to give a synopsis of the talk on the part of the Indians.

(Objected to by a member of the court, on the ground that it must all have been interpreted, and the interpreter was not under oath at the time. The judge-advocate remarked that no doubt that was the fact, but that in his opinion it was better to admit Mr. Meacham's account of what the Indians said in reply to General Canby and Doctor Thomas. It was thereupon decided to admit it for what it was worth. Objection withdrawn.)

Q. By judge-advocate. Well, Mr. Meacham, what did the Indians say?—A. The substance of Jack's speech was that he wanted the soldiers taken away. That was the main point. Schonchin John's speech was that he wanted Fairchild's ranch, or Hot Creek; these were the main points.

Q. Then what came?—A. The reply was that the President had sent the soldiers there, and that they could not be taken away without his consent.

Q. Who said that?—A. I think I said that myself, and that General Canby repeated it; that they were sent there by the President and could not be removed, without his consent. Schonchin John said he was willing to accept Hot Creek for a home; that he had been informed that he could have that place. He was asked, " Who told you you could have it ? Did Fairchilds or Dorris ?" He replied they did not, but from other sources he had learned he could have that place." Then Schonchin John said : " Unless the soldiers are taken away and you give us Hot Creek or Fairchild's ranch, we don't want to talk any more."

The interpreter had rendered that speech of Schonchin John's, or pretty nearly, perhaps not quite, finished it, when the two men sprang up. When the men came in sight, we all rose to our feet except Mrs. Riddle, who, I think, threw herself flat on the ground. While Schonchin was talking, Captain Jack had risen and turned his back and was walking off a few steps, perhaps behind Mr. Dyer's horse, or toward it ; he was coming again toward the circle at the time the Indians rose up ; he was rather facing it, but when the Indians made their appearance I asked the question of Captain Jack, " What does that mean ?" but he made no reply to me directly ; he put his right hand under the left breast pocket and drew his pistol, and sung out some word in Indian that I did not then understand.

Q. Had you seen the pistols before ?—A. I had seen the shape of them, not the pistols themselves ; I became satisfied they were all armed some time before that.

Q. You think the two men who appeared from the rocks came into sight before the first pistol was fired ?—A. I know it, sir.

Q. You saw them come out ?—A. Yes.

Q. What next took place ?—A. Captain Jack and Schonchin John changed places, bringing Captain Jack in front of General Canby and Schonchin in front of me ; and Captain Jack drew his pistol and the cap bursted but did not discharge.

Q. Whom did he aim at ?—A. At General Canby, and within less than three feet—pointed toward General Canby's head.

Q. Had the commissioners done anything to justify or excite the attack ?—A. There had been no angry words.

Q. Or motions?—A. No acts of any kind that could have provoked hostilities that I know of; on the contrary, we were sedulously careful to avoid it; and I believe we all appreciated the necessity of being careful in our conversation and in our action. But after the assault of Captain Jack with the pistol on General Canby, what I remember most distinctly was that Schonchin John drew his pistol from this (left) side of him.

Q. You saw it?—A. Yes ; within not to exceed 3 or 4 feet from me ; he discharged it at me, aiming evidently at my head. After drawing the pistol, almost at the same time or very nearly, he drew a knife which he held in his left hand.

Q. Did he hit you ?—A. Not at that time. He subsequently did shoot me. This ball which struck me in my face (showing) was discharged from the pistol in the hands of Schonchin John, within 15 or 16 feet of me, after I had taken the cover of a rock.

Q. Did you notice whether there was any more firing ?—A. There was ; the firing was very hot and they were all very active, making hostile demonstrations on the peace-commission party. One man was after Dyer I know, but I cannot tell who.

Q. You saw that ?—A. Yes ; I saw Dyer running and Riddle running, and I saw some men chasing him ; but I cannot designate the men who did it, only they were of the party who were in the council.

Q. Did you still retain your senses after this ball had struck you in the forehead ?—A. For a very short time afterward. Very soon afterward I received a shot in my wrist, and within a few seconds after I lost my consciousness, probably from the grazing shot on my temple. I remained unconscious until the skirmish-line of rescuers came up.

Q. What other wounds did you have?—A. I received a shot on my left hand, my right wrist, my face, the end of my ear and side of my head, and a knife-cut of four or five inches in length on the side of my head, besides bruises.

Q. Do you say the party of Indians, as soon as Jack fired, sprang simultaneously up?—A. Sprang up and commenced firing; all drew arms, or they were all engaged in it some way. I didn't see General Canby after Captain Jack had cocked his pistol to shoot the second time—I have no recollection of seeing him. I did see Dr. Thomas after he had received the first shot, and my memory is that Boston was shooting at him. Dr. Thomas got on his right hand without falling entirely to the ground.

Q. After this did you become unconscious?—A. Yes. I fell back thirty or forty steps from where the firing began; I succeeded in running that distance.

Q. When did you recover your senses?—A. When the skirmish-line, Colonel Miller's command, came up. I suppose it must have been the time that it required to march from headquarters on double-quick. I came to consciousness when the line came up, hearing the voice of Colonel Miller straightening his line; that is the first sound I remember.

Q. Do you have any doubt that the Indians intended to kill and murder you?—A. None.

Q. Did you ever receive this telegram?—A. I did.

The prisoners were then severally asked if they desired to cross-examine; to which they each replied in the negative.

Q. By commission. Were the Indians armed who were secreted in the rocks, and who came forward during the conference?—A. They were, with guns.

Q. By commission. Did those Indians who came from the rocks make their appearance before, or after, Captain Jack left his place and went to the rear?—A. After he started to go to the rear.

Q. By commission. Do you understand that Jack's going to the rear was a signal to those Indians hiding in the rocks to come out with their guns?—A. I have always so supposed it to be—to have been the signal; I believe it to have been.

Q. By judge-advocate. Had General Canby a weapon on his person?—A. Not that I am aware of.

Q. Had Dr. Thomas?—A. I know he had not.

Q. Were there any weapons in the party which could have been seen by the Indians?—A. I think not.

All the foregoing testimony was faithfully interpreted to the prisoners.

The judge-advocate then submitted to the commission the telegram referred to above and identified by Mr. Meacham, and also another attached to the first, both verified under the signature of the Secretary of the Interior, and the seal of the Department attached to record, and marked A. The judge-advocate stated that he offered them by way of additional proof of the position, as peace commissioner, held by Dr. Thomas.

The commission thereupon adjourned to meet at 9.30 a. m. to-morrow morning.

H. P. CURTIS,
Major, U. S. A., Judge-Advocate Commission.

FOURTH DAY.

FORT KLAMATH, OREG., *July 8, 1873—9.30 a. m.*
The commission met pursuant to adjournment.

Present: All the members named in the detail, and the judge-advocate, and the prisoners.

Proceedings of previous meeting were then read and approved.

H. R. ANDERSON, lieutenant Fourth Artillery, called for prosecution, duly sworn, testified as follows:

Question. By Judge-Advocate. What is your name and rank?—Answer. H. R. Anderson ; lieutenant Fourth Artillery.

Q. What position did you hold at the time of the death of General Canby ?—A. Personal aid and acting assistant adjutant-general, on General Canby's staff.

Q. What position did General Canby occupy at that time ?—A. He was then—two months' time of the negotiations—in command of the Military Division of the Pacific.

Q. Up to what date ?—A. I think up to the 6th of April he was in command of the Military Division ; after that, General Schofield returned and relieved him of the command.

Q. What command did he hold, if any, at the time of his death ?—A. Department of the Columbia, and adviser to the peace commission under telegraphic instructions from Washington.

Q. Was he in receipt of instructions from any source as to the course he was to pursue ; was he receiving instructions from time to time ?—A. Yes, sir, from time to time; from commanding General of the Army.

Q. What kind of instructions were they? Did you see them yourself ?—A. Yes, sir; generally telegraphic instructions.

Q. What was their nature? What did they instruct him to do ?—A. Instructed him to use his utmost endeavors to bring about a peaceable termination of the trouble.

Q. What relation did he hold with the peace commissioners ?—A. He was ordered down there to consult and advise with them.

Q. Do you remember General Canby's initials ?—A. E. R. S.; his full name was Edward Richard Sprigg Canby.

Q. In acting as he did in connection with the peace commissioners, whom did he represent ?—A. The United States Government.

Q. At the time he was killed what military operations, if any, were going on ?—A. None whatever.

Q. He was not alone there negotiating with the Indians ?—A. No, sir; there were troops encamped within two miles on one side and about three on the other, of Captain Jack's stronghold.

Q. Were there hostile forces on both sides ?—A. I don't know whether they were considered hostile at the negotiations or not ; they had been; no peace had been made; there were only negotiations going on, and cessation of hostilities.

Q. How do you know there had been hostilities ?—A. From official reports of the officers engaged with the Indians ; and the report of killed and wounded.

Q. How many engagements had there been ?—A. There had been two general engagements with the troops, and one or two skirmishes.

Q. Had there been lives lost and blood shed ?—A. Yes, sir ; I think some twenty-two or twenty-three killed, and died from wounds.

Q. What were the arms of the service, employed on the side of the United States ?—A. Up to that time they were cavalry and infantry.

Q. Where were the enemy?—A. A part of the time in Southern Oregon, and a part of the time in Northern California, in the vicinity of the lava-beds.

Q. Were they accessible in the lava-beds?—A. Yes, sir.

Q. Could they be got at?—A. Yes, sir.

Q. Were they entrenched?—A. Yes, sir; they had fortified themselves in the rocks in some places.

Q. How do you characterize the contest that was going on?—A. An Indian war.

Q. At the time of General Canby's death, I think you said, a suspension of arms and hostilities were existing?—A. Yes, sir.

Q. What led to the meeting of General Canby and the commissioners with the Indians—the last meeting?—A. A message from Captain Jack.

Q. Did he ask that, to your knowledge?—A. Yes, sir.

Q. Do you desire to make any further statement?—A. No, sir; except to say that the troops had moved after the first negotiations of peace—the peace commissioners; from Fairchilds, they had entirely broken off, and a movement of troops had taken place during the time that there was no communication between the Indians and the peace commissioners, which I think was some eight or ten days. The troops moved up, and then there were messages sent in from the commissioners desiring to have a talk; and they had a talk.

Q. Did you see General Canby dead?—A. No, sir.

Q. Or Dr. Thomas?—A. No, sir.

Q. About how long had these hostilities lasted which you speak of, between the United States force and this tribe; up to the time of the death of General Canby?—A. About five months.

Q. Did they terminate with his decease?—A. No, sir.

Q. Do you know of your own knowledge that there were engagements afterwards?—A. No, sir.

The judge-advocate here asked the prisoners, severally, if they desired to cross-examine the witness; to which they replied in the negative.

The commission had no question.

The above questions and answers were faithfully interpreted to the prisoners.

HENRY C. McELDERY, assistant surgeon U. S. A., called for prosecution, sworn; testified as follows:

Question. By judge-advocate. Did you see the body of General Canby after his decease?—A. I did sir; I saw it on the field on the evening of April 11.

Q. Was the General dead?—A. Yes, sir; he was quite dead when I saw him.

Q. Please describe his condition?—A. He had been entirely stripped of every article of clothing. He had three wounds on his body, and several abrasions of the face. One of the wounds, apparently made by a ball, was about at the inner canthus of the left eye. The edges of that wound were depressed, as if the ball had entered there.

Q. What is your opinion as to the cause of his death?—A. I think the gunshot wound of the head caused his death; this ball, which entered in the eye and came up in the head, and fractured the left parietal bone and went through the brain.

Q. He died of the wounds received by him, then, on the evening of the 11th?—A. Yes, sir.

Q. Did you see Dr. Thomas's body?—A. I saw him. There were several gunshot wounds in his body, but I don't recollect sufficient to swear to the exact locality of each one.

Q. What was your opinion as to the cause of his death?—A. I think the gunshot wound over his heart was the cause of his death.

Q. Did he die of wounds received on that day?—A. I think the wounds that I saw were sufficient to cause his death; yes, sir.

Q. Where were you employed during the war with the Modoc tribe?—A. I was an assistant surgeon under the United States Government; and was acting as chief medical officer at that time to the Modoc expedition.

Q. Chief medical officer of the force there?—A. Yes, sir.

Q. Did the war terminate with the death of General Canby?—A. No, sir.

Q. Were there other subsequent engagements?—A. Yes, sir.

Q. Were you present at any engagements which preceded the death of General Canby?—A. Yes, sir; I was in the affair on Lost River with Captain Jackson; the first affair.

Q. On what date?—A. That was on the 29th of November, 1872.

Q. Any others?—A. I was in the fight of General Wheaton on the 17th of January. I believe those are the only two.

Q. Were there lives lost?—A. Yes, sir.

The judge-advocate then asked the prisoners if they desired to cross-examine the witness; to which they replied in the negative.

Question. By the commission. Do I understand the witness to say he saw General Canby's body on the field?—A. Yes, sir.

The witness then corrected his testimony as follows: The gunshot wound causing the death of Dr. Thomas was of the heart; not merely over the heart.

The above questions and answers were severally interpreted to the prisoners.

The judge-advocate then offered to the commission extracts from General Orders No. 100, of the War Department, Adjutant-General's Office, Washington, April 24th, 1863, entitled " Instructions for the Government of armies in the field;" copy of which extracts are attached to the record and marked B.

The above were interpreted to the prisoners.

The judge-advocate then announced the testimony for the prosecution closed.

TESTIMONY FOR DEFENSE.

SCAR-FACED CHARLEY, an Indian, called for the defense; is cautioned against committing perjury, sworn, and testified as follows through the interpreter:

Question. By Captain Jack, (through the interpreter.) Tell about Link-River Jack coming and giving us powder and stuff.—Answer. The first time was down here at Ellen's, at the east end of the lava-bed; we were attacked there by the soldiers, and there were some Klamath Lake Indians along with the soldiers there, and they told us not to shoot at them but to shoot at the soldiers; the Klamaths did. We were all speaking of the Modoc tribe; I and my band. We killed one soldier down close to Louis Land's, at the east end of the lava-bed, when they were coming from Fort Bidwell, I believe.

Q. When was this?—A. That was directly after the fight at Lost River. The Klamath Lake Indians told me that they did not expect to be friends to the soldiers all of the time; that they would be our friends after a while; after that then they came with the soldiers to our strong-hold in the lava-bed and fought us; the Klamath Lake Indians did. In the fight there were ten of them came to us, and they gave us most of the ammunition we had; we took some of it and some of it was given to us; the Modocs got it from the Klamath Lakes; one in particular, "One-eye" or "Link-River Jack," gave us ammunition and guns. They got back one gun from us. They came to talk with us, and Scar-Faced Charley got eighty caps from one Klamath Lake Indian. They bought them of the Klamaths. The Klamath Lakes said to us "Don't shoot us, shoot the soldiers and let us alone: we are your friends." The Klamath Lakes told me that Allen David told them, when they went, to shoot up in the air. They said, "I don't want to shoot any of you; I listened to what Allen David told me; I held up my gun and I didn't want to shoot at any of you." That is what the Klamath Lakes said. One-eye Link-River gave Captain Jack twenty caps. One-eye Link-River then gave his powder-horn full of powder to Indian George, a Modoc; he poured it all out and gave it all to him that was in his horn. My tribe took a gun and one pistol away from them, and the reason of it was that they had stolen our horses and taken them away; the Klamath Lakes had. I never knew of Allen David telling the Indians to murder General Canby. I came up on the 11th of April, after the commissioners were killed. I was speaking of the powder and caps. Our tribe caught Little John and took him to our camp. Little John talked a long time to us and told us not to fight them; that they never would fight the Modocs. The day before the fight of January 17th, Little John told me to fight hard the next day and whip the soldiers and kill all we could; that Allen David had told him to tell us so, and to shoot up in the air and not to shoot at the Indians that were with the soldiers; that is Allen David. We said to Little John, "Don't you lie to us; you are the first ones who have tried to raise a fight and now you come and tell us you are our friends, to come and fight the soldiers." Little John said, "I don't lie; Allen Dave sent me here with this message." The whole tribe was there on one of these occasions. No white men ever told us to fight. Little Link-River John told me the Indians on the Yanax reservation were mad at us and wanted to kill us all. That they never wanted to see us any more. Schonchis never advised us to fight; Schonchis of the Yainax reservation, I mean; not this one, he would not talk with us. Link-River John told us that the Indians at Yanax were all afraid, but, that the Klamath Lakes were not afraid, and advised us to fight. I have never seen Modoc Sally. The way we got the most of our ammunition was after the fight of the 17th January last; we went round and picked up the cartridges; and the Klamath Lakes gave us some; and we opened the cartridges and got out the powder and then made bullets out of the lead in them. We had plenty of caps. In the fight of the 17th the Klamaths laid down, and after the soldiers moved on then I came to them and asked them who was their chief, and they told me that Link-River John was. There is where they gave us this ammunition and stuff. They said they came there to lay down behind the rocks to see us so they could get a chance to give us ammunition and powder. After the soldiers quit fighting, we were then going home to our strong-hold, all going along together, and we saw three Indians lying down behind the rocks; this was after they had given us the powder. The Klamath Lakes told us not to shoot them, that they were our friends; and I drew my pistol out and told them that they were the cause of the fight, that they had urged it on; and they said no, that they were always our friends. We had a long talk. I told them then to leave all the ammunition that they had and could get; to pile it under a rock there where we were and I would get it. I told them, " You say you are our friends and I want to see whether you are or not." "To see whether you will leave your cartridges and things here for us or not." I went the next day and found the ammunition there. There was a flour-sack half full; I got one hundred rounds of ammunition myself that they had left there. I then asked the Klamaths if they were telling the truth, and they said they were; that Allen David had told them to tell me that they would not fight us; that when they went there they went to shoot up to make the soldiers believe they were our enemies, but they were our friends. That is all I know.

Captain Jack said that he had no other questions to ask this witness. The judge-advocate had no questions to put.

Q. By commission. Where were you at the time of the massacre of the peace commissioners? Locate your position as near as possible.— A. At the time they began firing I was around at the bend of the lake, about half a mile away.

Q. By commission. Which, if any, of these prisoners were present with the peace commissioners at the time of the massacre?—A. George was one—Boston, Captain Jack, Hooker Jim, Bogus Charley. There were seven started out from the cave. Sconchis was there, and Shacknasty Jim. After Captain Jack and his band started, Barncho and Sloluck started and came out.

Q. By commission. Could you see the Indians firing on the commissioners?—A. I saw Captain Jack get up and walk back, and then after that I heard firing and saw them running.

Q. By commission. Whom do you mean by "them?"—A. Captain Jack and his band.

DAVE, a Modoc, called for defense, warned of the penalties of lying, duly sworn.

Question. By Captain Jack, (through interpreter.) What do you know about Lalake, and what he done?—Answer. Lalake, Klamath sub-chief, told me at Fairchild's that Allen David had told him to tell the Modocs to fight, and not to give up to the soldiers—not to make peace. Allen David's Indians all listened to him, and done what he said for them to do. I saw Lalake at Fairchild's. Lalake, and Modoc Sally and her man, came there while Meacham was there. I went into the house where he was, and Lalake came and asked me to shake hands. It was a good while before I would shake hands with him. He said, "I came here to see you all; I want to talk with you. I have been up to Yanax, and have had a talk, and tried to get a pass to come here, but I could not." Lalake asked me, "Why don't some of you come over and have a talk? Allen David said he didn't know what was the matter that we didn't come to have a talk." Lalake told me that Allen David said he wanted to know who was our big chief—Sconchis or Jack—"that he was ashamed that he had not seen anything of them; that his heart was with us, and he told us never to give up to the soldiers, but to fight." Allen David sent this message to Jack and his people through Lalake, that he was ashamed that he had not told the Modocs before, and made arrangements with them before the Lost River fight, in 1872, so that he might have been with them and helped them out. Lalake told me that some white man had told the Klamaths that Captain Jack had burnt one of the Klamaths. Allen David sent Captain Jack a message then, and wanted to know why he had made his, David's, message known so soon. He was ashamed that after he had sent him as good talk as he had, that he had told it. Why didn't he keep it a secret? He said, "The Klamaths are your friends and have given you ammunition, and will give it you whenever you want it."

Captain Jack had no further questions to put the witness.

The judge-advocate declined to cross-examine.

The commission had no questions to put.

ONE-EYED MOSE, Indian, called for the defense, warned of the penalties of perjury; sworn; testified as follows:

Captain JACK. Tell about Link River Jack?—Answer. I saw Link River Jack a little south of where the first fight took place on Lost River; I had two squaws with me. Link River Jack came there and wanted to see some one; he wanted, he said, to be a friend to us. After he seen us he told us the soldiers were close by, and for us to leave; this was the same day of the Lost River fight. Another Indian, Link River One-Eye, came and asked us if we had any caps, and we told him we didn't have many. He gave me seven; he gave Barncho seven caps, and George twenty-seven; he then gave us powder that he had.

Captain JACK stated he had no further testimony to elicit from this witness.

The judge-advocate declined to cross-examine.

The commission had no questions to ask.

The judge-advocate then inquired of each prisoner successively if they had any witnesses to summon. Jack having stated that he had no more witnesses to summon, each replied in the negative.

Captain JACK thereupon made the following address to the commission, through interpreter:

I will talk about Judge Roseborough first; he always told me to be a good man; he said, "I know the white man's heart, but not the Indian's heart so well." Roseborough never gave me any advice but good advice. I have known a great many white people; I have known there was a great many of them had good hearts; I don't know all of the Indian chiefs around, and I don't know what their hearts were. Judge Roseborough told me to be a good man, and do the right thing by my fellow-man. I considered myself as a white man; I didn't want to have an Indian heart any longer; I took passes from good white men who gave me good advice. I knew all the people that were living about the country, and they all knew I was an honest man, and that I always acted right, nor did anything wrong. You men here don't know what I have been heretofore; I never accused any white man of being mean and bad; I always thought them my friends, and when I went to any one and asked him for a pass, he would always give it to me; all gave me passes, and told those people who had to pass through my country that I was a good Indian, and had never disturbed anybody. No white man can say that I ever objected to their coming to live in my country; I always told them to come and live there, and that I was willing to give them homes there. I would like to see the man that ever knew me to do anything wrong heretofore; I have always dealt upright and honest with every man; nobody ever called me mean, except the Klamath Indians; I never knew any other chief who spoke in favor of the white men as I have done, and I have always taken their part, and spoken in favor of them; I was always advised by good men in Yreka, and about there, to watch over white men when traveling through my country, and I have taken their advice and always done it. I would like to see the man who started this fuss, and caused me to be in the trouble I am in now.

They scared me when they came to where I was living on Lost River, and started this fight. I cannot understand why they were mad with me. I have always told the white man heretofore to come and settle in my country; that it was his country and Captain Jack's country. That they could come and live there with me and that I was not mad with them. I have never received anything from anybody, only what I bought and paid for myself. I have always lived like a white man, and wanted to live so. I always tried to live peaceably and never asked any man for anything. I have always lived on what I could kill and shoot with my gun, and catch in my trap. Riddle knows that I have always lived like a man, and have never gone begging; that what I have got, I have always got with my own hands, honestly. I should have taken his advice. He has always given me good advice, and told me to live like a white man; and I have always tried to do it, and did do it until this war started. I hardly know how to talk here. I don't know how white people talk in such a place as this; but I will do the best I can.

The judge-advocate. Talk exactly as if you were at home, in a council.

JACK, continuing. I have always told white men when they came to my country, that if they wanted a home to live there they could have it; and I never asked them for any pay for living there as my people lived. I liked to have them come there and live. I liked to be with white people. I didn't know anything about the war—when it was going to commence. Major Jackson came down there and commenced on me while I was in bed asleep. When Meacham came to talk to me, he always came and talked good to me. He never talked about shooting, or anything of that kind. It was my understanding that Ivon Applegate was to come and have a talk with me, and not to bring soldiers, but to come alone. I was ready to have a talk with any man that would come to talk peace with me. The way I wanted that council with Applegate to come off, was, I wanted Henry Miller to be there and hear it. He always talked good to me and gave me good advice. Miller told me he wanted to talk with me, and wanted to be there when Applegate met me, and wanted to talk for me and with me. Dennis Crawley told me he wanted to be there to talk with me when Applegate came. He told me I was a good man, and he wanted to see me get my rights. It scared me when Major Jackson came and got there just at daylight, and made me jump out of my bed without a shirt or anything else on. I didn't know what it meant, his coming at that time of day. When Major Jackson and his men came up to my camp, they surrounded it, and I hollered to Major Jackson for them not to shoot, that I would talk. I told Bogus Charley to go and talk, until I could get my clothes on. He went and told them that he wanted to talk; that he didn't want them to shoot. Then they all got down off their horses, and I thought then we were going to have a talk; and I went into another tent. I thought, then, why were they mad with me; what had they found out about me, that they came here to fight me. I went into my tent then and sat down and they commenced shooting. My people were not all there; there were but a few of us there. Major Jackson shot my men while they were standing round. I ran off; I did not fight any. I threw my people away that they had shot and wounded. I did not stop to get them. I ran off, and did not want to fight. They shot some of my women, and they shot my men. I did not stop to inquire anything about it, but left and went away. I went then into the lava-beds. I had very few people, and did not want to fight. I thought I had but few people, and it was not of any use for me to fight.

and so I went to the lava-beds. While I was on my way to the cave, there was a white man came to my camp. I told him the soldiers had pitched onto me, and fired into me while I was asleep, but I would not hurt him—for him to go back to town, home. I went into the lava-beds and staid there. I didn't go to any place, I did not want to fight, and I did not think about fighting any more. I didn't see any white men for a long time. I didn't want to kill anybody. I went to my cave and there I staid. John Fairchild came to my house, and asked me if I wanted to fight, and I said no, I had quit fighting, that I did not want to fight any more—him nor anybody. The Hot Creek Indians then started for the reservation and got as far as Bob Whittle's, on Klamath River, and there the Linkville men scared them and they ran back. They were going to kill them. Then the Hot Creeks came to my camp and told me the whites were going to kill them all. They got scared by what the white men had told them, that they were going to kill them all.

There were some of the Indians I left at Fairchild's; they were talking about bringing them by the way of Lost River. They ran off too. When they all got to my place I told some of them to go back to Fairchild's. The Hot Creek Indians came from the other side and came to my place. Hooker Jim came from this side, the east side of Lost River or Tule Lake, and they came around the lower end of Tule Lake and came to my place. I didn't know anything of any settlers being killed until Hooker Jim came with his band and told me. I didn't think that they would kill the whites when they went around that way. I did not believe it. I did not want them to stay with me. None of my people had killed any of the whites, and I had never told Hooker Jim and his party to murder any settlers; and I did not want them to stay with me. I don't know who told them to kill the settlers. I always advised them *not* to kill white people. I told Hooker that I never had killed any white person, and never had advised him to kill them; that he killed them of his own accord, not from my advice. I thought all of the white men liked me that was living in my country. I always thought they did. They always treated me well. (To Hooker Jim:) What did you kill those people for? I never wanted you to kill my friends. You have done it on your own responsibility.

Then I thought that, after hearing that those white people had been killed, that the whites would all be mad at me. And it troubled me and made me feel bad. I told them it was bad, and they ought not to have done it. I knew that the white people would be mad at me just on account of this Hooker Jim killing so many white people when he had no business to do it. After I had left Lost River, I had quit then, and I had not fought any, and did not intend to fight any more. Fairchilds told me that that was bad; that they had killed the settlers; that it was wrong; and if they did not quit fighting there, the chances were the soldiers would all come on us again and kill us all, if we did not make peace then. I told Fairchilds that I did not want to fight any more; that I was willing to quit if the soldiers would quit. Fairchilds then never came to my house any more for a long time after the Indians that were stopping with him had run off. He was afraid to come then any more. It was a long time that I heard nothing from him. Nobody came to my place, and I could not get any news. After a great while Fairchilds came again with a squaw, and told me I had better make peace, for the white people were all mad at us. For a good while then there was nothing going on, and again the soldiers came there. When the soldiers came they came fighting and fought all day. The first day the soldiers got there they fought a little; the next day, all day. The soldiers came and they fought a part of two days and then went away again.

Link River John came and told me not to be mad at them. I told them that I never had killed anybody and never wanted to. When Fairchilds came in to see me I told him I was not mad at anybody, and did not want to fight, and did not want any more war. I told Fairchilds I did not know what they were mad with me about; that I was willing to quit fighting; willing for both sides to quit it and live again in peace. I told him that I did not want the Lost River country any more; that as there had been trouble about that, I wanted to go to some place else and live, and did not want to live there any more. I told them there had been blood spilt there on Lost River, and that I did not want to live there; that I would hunt some other place and live; and that I was willing to quit fighting if they would let me alone. I do not deny telling Fairchilds, or anybody else, that I wanted to talk good talk. I always wanted to talk good talk. I wanted to quit fighting. My people were all afraid to leave the cave. They had been told that they were going to be killed, and they were afraid to leave there: and my women were afraid to leave there. While the peace talk was going on there was a squaw came from Fairchilds and Dorris's, and told us that the peace commissioners were going to murder us. That they were trying to get us out to murder us. A man by the name of Nate Beswick told us so. There was an old Indian man came in the night and told us again.

The INTERPRETER. That is one of those murdered in the wagon while prisoners by the settlers.

CAPTAIN JACK, (continuing.) This old Indian man told me that Nate Beswick told him that that day Meacham, General Canby, Dr. Thomas, and Dyer were going to murder us if we came at the council. All of my people heard this old man tell us so. And then there was another squaw came from Fairchilds and told me that Meacham and the peace commissioners had a pile of wood ready built up, and were going to burn me on this pile of wood; that when they brought us into Dorris's they were going to burn me there. All of the squaws about Fairchilds and Dorris's told me the same thing. After hearing all th s news I was afraid to go, and that is the reason I did come in to make peace.

Riddle and his woman always told me the truth, and advised me to do good, but I have never taken their advice. If I had listened to them instead of to the squaws, that were lying all of the time, I would not have been in the fix that I am in now.

The reason that I did not come when the wagons came after me was, this squaw had come the night before and told me they were going to burn me, and I was afraid to come. I can see now that the squaws at Fairchild's and Dorris's were lying to me all the time; and Bob Whittles's wife lied to me. If I had listened to Riddle I would have been a heap better off. Bob Whittles's came to see me and she told me that I was not her people, and she did not want to talk anything good to me. She always gave me bad advice. She told me that if she did not come back again right straight, that I might know the soldiers would be on to me the next day to fight me.

I have told you about the advice that I heard and the main cause of my never coming in and making peace. I was afraid to come. I don't consider myself, when you came to have a talk with me, the chief then. When you, and the reporters came in the cave with you, I didn't know what to say; I didn't know anything about fighting then, and didn't want to fight. Your chief makes his men mind him and listen to him, and they do listen to what he tells them, and they believe him; but my people won't. My men would not listen to me. They wanted to fight. I told them not to fight. I wanted to talk and make peace and live right; but my men would not listen to me. The men that were in the cave with me never listened to what I said; and they cannot one of them say, and tell the truth, that I ever advised them to fight. I have always told my people to keep out of trouble; that when I met in council I wanted to meet in peace and in a friendly way. I told them when they would not listen to me, that if they wanted to fight, and would fight, they would have to fight; but they would not do so from anything that I told them; that it was against my will to fight.

By my being the chief of the Modoc tribe, I think that the white people all think that I raised the fight and kept it going. I have told my people that I thought the white people would think that about me; and I didn't want to have anything to do with it; that if they wanted to fight they would have to go on their own hook.

Hooker Jim was one that agitated the fighting: that wanted to fight all of the time. I sat over to one side with my few men and did not say anything about fighting. Now I have to bear the blame for him and the rest of them.

Schonchis was with Hooker Jim; he was on Hooker Jim's side. I was by myself with my few men that I had, and did not have anything to say. They were all mad at me. Then I would think that the white people would think that I was the cause of all this fuss; and then I would think again that they surely could not think so, when they knew that these other men had committed these murders. I would talk to them, but they would not listen to me. I told them that I liked my wife and my children, and I did not want any trouble, but wanted to live in peace; but they would not listen to what I would say. I had not done anything. I had not shot anybody. I never commenced the fight. Hooker Jim is the one that always wanted to fight, and commenced killing and murdering. When I would get to talking they would tell me to hush! that I didn't know anything; that I was nothing more than an old squaw. I and Hooker Jim had a fuss, and I told him that I had not done anything mean; that he had been murdering the settlers. And I got my revolver, and if I could have seen him through the canvas I would have killed him. I thought that I would kill him; and I wanted to kill him, for he is the one that murdered the settlers on Tule Lake. I thought that the white people were mad because I was living on Lost River, and that they wanted that land there; that is what I thought when the fight commenced. I then had a fuss with another Indian because I got mad at Hooker Jim—an Indian called George. George and I had a quarrel, and he told me I was nothing but an old squaw; that I never had killed anybody; that he had killed white people and had killed lots of soldiers—him and Hooker Jim. Hooker Jim said, "You are like an old squaw; you have never done any fighting yet; we have done the fighting, and you are our chief. You are not fit to be a chief." I told him that I was not ashamed of it; that I knew I had not killed anybody, and I did not want to kill anybody, and I would have felt sorry if I had killed any white people. They told me that I was laying around in camp and did not do anything, but lay there like a log, and they were traveling around and killing people and stealing things. That they, Hooker and George, were not afraid to travel. They said "What do you want with a gun? you don't shoot anything with it. You don't go any place to do anything. You are sitting around on the rocks." I told them that I knew and was not ashamed to be called an old squaw; that I thought I done my duty by telling them to keep the peace; but they would not listen to me. I told them that they run around and committed these murders against my will. Scar-faced Charley told me that he would go with Hooker and them; that he could fight with them; that I was nothing but an old squaw. I told them then if that was what they were going to do, why they could go on their own responsibility; that I did not want to go with them; that I did not want to live with them. Scar-faced Charley will tell everything that he knows. He don't want to keep anything back; neither do I want to keep anything back.

Captain JACK then requested to be allowed to suspend further remarks, and to continue to-morrow, which request was granted.

SCHONCHIS being asked by the judge-advocate if he had anything to say, made the following remarks:

When I was camped on Lost River I was scared by the soldiers. I was living there in peace, killing ducks. I was out ducking, and I looked over and I could see them fighting. It scared me, and I wondered what was the matter. I looked on each side of me, and I saw the fire on each side, and I wondered what was the matter; this was the first fight on Lost River, in November, 1872. I seen the fire on each side of me, and I started for the fire. I wondered to myself if the soldiers and Indians were fighting, and wondered what it was about; and wondered who was the cause of the fight, and how the fight could take place there, and why the soldiers came to kill my children. I wondered where a chief could come from that was mad with me. I didn't know why they should come to fight me and my children. I saw the Indians putting their guns and their wounded Indians into a canoe. When I got to where the fight had taken place, the Indians had all gone. I wondered who had set the grass afire there or the houses. I wondered what they wanted to burn up my house for. I started then for the mountains. I went to hunt my family. I overtook Hooker Jim in the mountain; I told him not to go. Hooker Jim told me that there were two of our men killed. Hooker Jim was very mad, and kept on in the mountains. I told him not to fight, but to go to the mountains and stay there. I told him to make haste and get into the mountains. I followed him for a long ways, and talked to him until I got beyond a little hill down on Tule Lake, and then I quit talking to him there. Hooker Jim seen four white men there. I didn't see them. I was afoot; Hooker Jim and three or four others were riding. They went on down to the lake. There I left them, and didn't know what they had done. After Hooker Jim and I had parted, my son then went and followed Hooker up. I told him not to go. I went out to one side and sat down on a log, and sat there for a long time. I looked over toward Lost River, and seen the soldiers coming. When I seen the soldiers coming I struck out for the mountains. Then I came down off of the mountains and went on to the flat of Tule Lake. I met Curly-Headed Doctor down in the settlement where the whites were living, after he had killed the settlers. I talked to them, and told them not to do it; but they would not listen to me. I went down toward the east end of Tule Lake and saw two white men. I have no more to say.

The judge-advocate then asked the remaining prisoners severally if they had anything to say, to which they replied in the negative.

The court then adjourned to meet at 9½ a. m. the following day, July 9th.

H. P. CURTIS,
Major, Judge-Advocate U. S. A.,
Judge-Advocate Military Commission.

178   MODOC WAR.

FIFTH DAY.

FORT KLAMATH, OREGON, *July* 9, 1873.

The commission met according to adjournment

Present, all the members named in the detail, the judge-advocate, and the prisoners.

The proceedings of the last meeting were read and approved.

CAPTAIN JACK, prisoner, continued his remarks to the commission as follows :

The four scouts have told you they didn't know anything about the murder of General Canby ; and they advocated the murder of General Canby with me. The Indians that told that the talk took place in my house about the murder of General Canby, lie. It was their own house it took place in. I don't want to keep anything back. I do not want to tell a lie about it. I would like to know why they told that they did not want to fight; or didn't say anything in regard to fighting. They all talked to me and were all in with it, because we didn't want to move off to any country that we didn't know anything about. I would like to know why Hooker Jim could not tell who he wanted to kill when he went out there. He says he went there to kill a man ; but he would not tell the man he wanted to kill. Meacham was the man that he wanted to kill. Them four scouts knew all about it ; and they were in our councils when we were holding councils, and they all wanted to kill the peace commissioners ; they all advised me to do it. I thought that it would all be laid on to me, and I wondered to myself if there could be any other man that it could be laid upon.

Another thing that made me afraid to meet the commissioners, the Indians lied to me and told me that Dr. Thomas and the other peace commissioners had pistols with them, and wanted to kill us. I told them that I didn't see any pistols with anybody, and they surely must have lied. I told them that I did not want to have any trouble with the peace commissioners ; that I did not want to kill them. Hooker Jim, he said that he wanted to kill Meacham, and we must do it. That is all I have got to say.

Here the testimony closed.

The judge-advocate then addressed the commission as follows :

I did not intend to say a single word in reference to the evidence, nor do I intend to now. But Captain Jack has cast some imputations upon the military and moral character of Major Jackson, which it seems to me to be my duty to do away with if I can.

Captain Jack states in his speech, that at the affair on Lost River, Major Jackson came upon him in the early morning and surprised him, and killed his women, and killed some of his men ; that he fired upon them without provocation, and so much to his surprise as to compel him to jump out of his bed without his shirt; and he expressed great surprise that the attack should have been made upon him. He says he wondered at the time why they should be mad at him.

It is a perfectly well-known fact that there is a treaty existing between the United States and the Modocs, by which the Modocs are obliged to remain upon the Yainox reservation ; and that this section of the band had been recreant to their duty, and had persisted in remaining off the reservation, very much to the annoyance, and, I might say, to the terror of the inhabitants of that region where they lived ; a terror which has been justified by subsequent events. Twice, I think, Mr.

Meacham was compelled to restore them to the reservation; and I understand, and I believe it is well known, that at the time of the Lost River affair, they were then persistently refusing to return to the reservation, and Mr. Odeneal, the then superintendent, found he must call upon the military to restore them to the reservation. They were in the wrong in remaining off the reservation, and in refusing to return. Major Jackson was thereupon directed, in compliance with the request of Mr. Odeneal to the post commander, Major Green, to go with his force and compel them to return.

The following is the order:

EXHIBIT C.

[Orders No. 937.]

HEADQUARTERS FORT KLAMATH, OREGON,
November 28, 1872.

In compliance with the request of the superintendent of Indian affairs for Oregon, dated Link River, November 27, 1872, Capt. James Jackson, First Cavalry, with all the available men of his troop, will proceed at once via Link River to Captain Jack's camp of Modoc Indians, endeavoring to get there before to-morrow morning, and if any opposition is offered on the part of the Modoc Indians to the requirements of the superintendent, he will arrest, if possible, Captain Jack, Black Jim, and Scar-faced Charley. He will endeavor to do all this without bloodshed, if possible, but if the Indians persist in refusing to obey the orders of the Government, he will use such force as may be necessary to compel them to do so, and the responsibility must rest on the Indians who defy the authority of the Government.

Captain Jackson is authorized to make any expenditures that may be necessary for the accomplishment of this object.

The post-quartermaster will send a pack-train with supplies to follow the troop, and he is authorized to hire such packers as may be necessary.

The troop will carry three days' rations on their saddles.

Assist. Surg. Henry McElderry and Lieutenant Boutelle, acting post-adjutant, will accompany the expedition.

By order of Maj. John Green:

F. A. BOUTELLE,
Second Lieutenant First Cavalry.

A true copy:

GEO. B. KINGSBURY,
Second Lieutenant Twelfth Infantry, Post-Adjutant.

This paper shows that the actions of Major Jackson were strictly in compliance with orders in enforcing the stipulations of the treaty, by compelling these Modocs to return to their reservation, which they had persistently refused to do.

In order to refute the imputations upon Major Jackson's character, which have been cast upon it by Captain Jack, as I believe most unjustly and falsely, I know no better way than reading the official report made by Major Jackson to Major Green, of the First Cavalry, commanding the post at Fort Klamath, on the 2d day of December, three days after the affair at Lost River. This is a duplicate of his official report, corrected and signed by Maj. James Jackson, himself, in my presence, a few days ago, and marked by him as a duplicate. It may be relied upon as absolutely accurate. It is an official report, and is therefore equivalent to a statement under oath, or nearly so. Whatever he says as coming under his own observation may be relied upon with absolute confidence, and is open to no possible dispute. Much of it is information received by him from others, it is true; but known to be not in any degree the less accurate for that reason.

180   MODOC WAR.

Exhibit D.

CAMP AT CRAWLEY'S RANCH,
Lost River, Oregon, December 2, 1872.

MAJOR: I sent you two days ago a hasty report of operations in the field. I have now the honor to submit a detailed report of my operations since I left Fort Klamath, Oregon. In compliance with your order No. 93, November 28, 1872, I moved from Fort Klamath, Oregon, at 11 o'clock a. m., with Lieutenant Boutelle, Dr. McElderry, thirty-six men of B Troop in column, and four with the pack-train.

Guided by Mr. Ivan Applegate, we marched all day and night through a heavy rain-storm, and arrived at the principal camp of the Modoc Indians about daylight. Forming line, I moved down on the camp at a trot, completely surprising the Indians, and creating great commotion among them. Halting just at the edge of the camp, I called to them to lay down their arms and surrender. I also got Mr. Applegate to interpret to them my intention, and ask them to comply with the orders of the Indian Department. Some of them seemed willing to do so, but Scar-faced Charley, Black Jim, and some others kept their guns, and commenced making hostile demonstrations against us. After repeated demands on them to lay down their arms and surrender had been unheeded, and seeing that the hostile Indians were getting more numerous and determined, I directed Lieutenant Boutelle to take some men from the line, and arrest the leader, if possible. This order was followed by firing on the part of the Indians, and a general engagement ensued. I poured in volley after volley among the worst men, killing the worst of them, capturing the camp, and driving the Indians to the refuge of the brush and hills, from whence they kept up a desultory fire for some little time.

I lost, during the engagement, and almost at the first fire, one man killed, and seven wounded, and one horse killed. After driving the Indians out of range, it became necessary to take care of the wounded to prevent the squaws remaining in camp from killing and mutilating them.

Leaving a slight skirmish-line in charge of Lieutenant Boutelle, I took what men could be spared and had the dead and wounded carried to the river-bank, and carried to Rawley's ranch, about half a mile below. I then dismantled the camp, capturing Jack's three rifles and his two saddles. All Indian guns found in camp were broken up or thrown into the river. At the same time that I arrived on the main camp of the Modocs, a smaller camp on the north side of the river was attacked by ten citizens, among them Mr. Oliver Applegate, Mr. O. T. Brown, of Linkville, Mr. Jack Burnett, of Radburg, Mr. Dennis Crawley, of Linkville, Mr. C. Monroe, of Linkville, Mr. Thurbur, Mr. Caldwell, and others; they also demanded the surrender of these Indians, which was not acceded to, and when the firing commenced on the main camp, they opened fire on the citizens and the citizens on them. One citizen (Mr. Thurber) was killed, and it is believed several Indians were killed and wounded. The citizens, after the first attack, retired to Mr. Crawley's ranch, and kept up the fire at long range, preventing the Indians from crossing the river and attacking my flank or rear. Two citizens coming up the road, and not knowing of the fight, were shot, one mortally and the other dangerously wounded. Soon after the fight, Mr. Applegate, Mr. Brown, Mr. Burnett, and some others, left to warn citizens in other places of danger, leaving but a small force at the house where my wounded had been sent, and where a family resided. Mr. Crawley rode up and asked for protection at the ranch, stating that the Indians were preparing for a new attack. I mounted the command and moved out at a trot for the ford, some eight miles up the river, sending Lieutenant Boutelle with a skirmish-line to clear the Indians out of the sage-brush, which he did effectually. It was between 3 and 4 o'clock when the troop arrived at the ranch, where we took post, to await supplies and care for the wounded. While moving around to the ranch, some straggling Indians collected on the other side of the river and burned a hay-stack and house belonging to Mr. Monroe; after this they moved out, down Tule Lake, for their refuge in the caves and rocks south of the lake. One band from the north side of the river, who had been fighting the citizens, moved down on that side of the lake during the fight, and commenced killing the unarmed inhabitants of Tule Lake Valley.

It was not until the next morning after the fight, while sending the wounded away in charge of the surgeon, that I learned there were any inhabitants near the scene of the conflict, or that they had been unwarned of approaching danger. I immediately sent a detachment with Mr. Crawley to ascertain the condition or fate of these people. He visited the first place, Mr. Boddy's, about three and a half miles below his (Mr. Crawley's) ranch, and found the house deserted, but everything in order, no sign of attack or murder, no tracks around the house, a dog tied to the door-step, and animals in the corral. Thinking, from appearances, that the family must have had warning and fled, believing that the warning had been carried down the valley, he came back and so reported.

That evening, November 30, I moved to the ford to meet the supply-train and prevent its being intercepted by prowling bands of Indians. The pack train came up at midnight, and the next morning, December 1, the command was moved back to Crawley's ranch for station until such time as supplies sufficient for a campaign could be collected. The evening of December 1, two citizens, residents of Tule Lake Valley, came in and reported that the men of the Boddy family had been murdered right after or during the fight by the band of Indians who had escaped, and that the women of the family had not been molested, but had walked across the mountains to Lost River bridge, and were then at Linkville.

Lieutenant Boutelle with a detachment was sent down with these men this morning, and some of the bodies of the Boddy family found in the timber, quite a distance from the house, where they had been cutting and hauling wood. The detachment was proceeding on down the valley, when they were met by Mr. Ivan Applegate, Mr. Langell, and some others who had come up the valley, visiting the ranches on the north side of the lake. They reported the killing of the men of the Brotherton family, (3,) two herders, and Mr. Henry Miller. Mrs. Brotherton and her two little boys had fought the Indians away from the house, wounding some of them; she with her three children, two boys and a little girl, came up with the party of citizens and soldiers, and are now at this station. Quite a party of citizens have collected here. To-morrow quite a large force will move down the valley to hunt up the remains of the murdered inhabitants. I send you a list of those known or supposed to have been killed: Mr. William Boddy, Rufus Boddy, William Boddy, jr., Nicholas Sheaver, William Brotherton, W. K. Brotherton, Rufus Brotherton, Christopher Erasmus, Robert Alexander, John Soper, —— Collins, Mr. Henry Miller.

I have sent a detachment to Clear Lake for the protection of Mr. Jesse Applegate's family, and will move the infantry you send me into Langell Valley and Clear Lake, the only places now threatened.

A company of Klamath Indians, thirty-six in number, commanded by Captain Farre, of Klamath Indian agency, came in to-day, and will go out on the trail of the Modocs to-morrow, to hunt them up and keep them from raiding until the troops can move upon their hiding-places. I think it will be necessary to make a depot of supplies at this point, as beyond this, in the direction the Indians have gone, wagons cannot be moved any distance, and the troops have to depend on a pack-train for supplies.

The troop behaved splendidly under fire, although a number of the men were raw recruits.

Doctor McElderry was present in the field during the fight, and I take great pleasure in recommending him and Lieutenant Boutelle for coolness, gallantry, and efficient service.

I am, sir, very respectfully, &c.,

JAMES JACKSON,
Captain First Cavalry, Commanding B Troop.

Maj. JOHN GREEN,
First Cavalry, Commanding Fort Klamath, Oregon.

The only portion of this official report upon which I rely is that containing Major Jackson's statements of what he himself saw. He touches at some length upon the massacres in Tule Lake or Lost River Valley in 1872, but, certain as it is that they took place, of them he *knows* nothing, as appears from his own account, or knows it only from information derived from eye-witnesses.

I do not accuse Captain Jack of any participation in those murders. I acquit him of them entirely. I know almost to a demonstration that he was ignorant of their occurrence until after they had taken place. I have investigated that matter somewhat since I have been here, and I do not believe he was concerned in them or knew of them in advance. Nor am I sure there exists sufficient legal testimony to identify the individuals of that party by whom that massacre was committed. I acquit Captain Jack of that. But when he accuses Captain Jackson of having acted in an unmilitary manner, by opening a fire upon him in his bed, and killing his women without notice, I deem it my duty, in vindication of Major Jackson's character, to submit to this commission the official report made by Major Jackson himself. I submit the case without further remark.

The commission was then closed for deliberation, and having maturely considered the evidence adduced, find the prisoner, known as Captain Jack, as follows:

Of the first specification, charge 1, " Guilty."
Of the second specification, charge 1, " Guilty."
Of charge 1, " Guilty."
Of first specification, charge 2, " Guilty."
Of second specification, charge 2, " Guilty."
Of charge 2, " Guilty."
And the commission does therefore sentence him, Captain Jack, to be hanged by the neck until he be dead, at such time and place as the proper authority shall direct; two-thirds of the members of the commission concurring therein.

And the commission do find the prisoner known as Schonchis as follows :
Of the first specification, charge 1, " Guilty."
Of the second specification, charge 1, " Guilty."
Of the first charge, " Guilty."
Of the first specification, charge 2, " Guilty."
Of the second specification, charge 2, " Guilty."
Of the second charge, " Guilty."
And the commission do therefore sentence him, Schonchis, to be hanged by the neck until he be dead, at such time and place as the proper authority may direct, two thirds of the members of the commission concurring therein.

And the commission do find the prisoner, Boston Charley, as follows :
Of specification 1, charge 1, " Guilty."
Of specification 2, charge 1, " Guilty."
Of charge 1, " Guilty."
Of specification 1, charge 2, " Guilty."
Of specification 2, charge 2, " Guilty."
Of charge 2, " Guilty."
And the commission do therefore sentence him, Boston Charley, to be hanged by the neck until he be dead, at such time and place as the proper authority shall direct, two-thirds of the members of the commission concurring therein.

And the commission do find the prisoner, Black Jim, as follows :
Of specification 1, charge 1, " Guilty."
Of specification 2, charge 1, " Guilty."
Of charge 1, " Guilty."
Of specification 1, charge 2, " Guilty."
Of specification 2, charge 2, " Guilty."
Of charge 2, " Guilty."
And the commission do sentence him, Black Jim, to be hanged by the neck until he be dead, at such time and place as the proper authority shall direct; two-thirds of the members of the commission concurring therein.

And the commission do find the prisoner, Barncho, as follows :
Of specification 1, charge 1, " Guilty."
Of specification 2, charge 2, " Guilty."
Of charge 1, " Guilty."
Of specification 1, charge 2, " Guilty."
Of specification 2, charge 2, " Guilty."
Of charge 2, " Guilty."
And the commission do therefore sentence him, Barncho, to be hanged by the neck until he be dead, at such time and place as the proper authority may direct; two-thirds of the members of the commission concurring therein:

And the commission do find the prisoner, Schloluck, or Cok, as follows :
Of specification 1, charge 1, " Guilty."
Of specification 2, charge 1, " Guilty."
Of charge 1, " Guilty."
Of specification 1, charge 2, " Guilty."
Of specification 2, charge 2, " Guilty."
Of charge 2, " Guilty."
And the commission does therefore sentence him, Scholuck, alias Cok, to be hanged by the neck until he be dead, at such time and place as the proper authority shall direct; two-thirds of the members concurring therein.

W. L. ELLIOTT,
Lieut.-Col. First Cavalry, President Mil. Com.
H. P. CURTIS,
Maj. U. S. A., Judge-Advocate Mil. Com.

The judge-advocate having informed the commission that he had no further business to bring before it, the commission adjourned *sine die.*

W. L. ELLIOTT,
Lieut.-Col. First Cavalry, President Mil. Com.
H. P. CURTIS,
Maj. U. S. A., Judge-Advocate Mil. Com.

The proceedings and findings of the military commission in the above cases of Captain Jack, Schonchis, Boston Charley, Black Jim, Barncho, Schloluck or Cok, Modoc Indian prisoners, are approved, and the sentences are confirmed. In compliance with War Department General Order No. 72, July 7, 1873, they are respectfully transmitted to the Bureau of Military Justice, to be laid before the President for his orders.

JEF. C. DAVIS,
Col. and Bvt. Maj.-Genl. U. S. A., Reviewing Officer.

JULY 29, 1873.

EXECUTIVE OFFICE, *August 22, 1873.*

The foregoing sentences in the cases of Captain Jack, Shonchis, Black Jim, Boston Charley, Barncho alias One-Eyed Jim, and Sloluck alias Cok, Modoc Indian prisoners, are hereby approved; and it is ordered that the sentences in the said cases be carried into execution by the proper military authority, under the orders of the Secretary of War, on the third day of October, eighteen hundred and seventy-three.

U. S. GRANT,
President.

WAR DEPARTMENT,
Washington, August 23, 1873.

The foregoing record of the proceedings in the trial by military commission of Captain Jack, Schonchis, Black Jim, Boston Charley, Barncho alias One-Eyed Jim, and Sloluck alias Cok, Modoc Indian prisoners, having been transmitted to the President and laid before him for his orders thereon ;.and the President having in the foregoing orders approved the sentences and directed that they be executed under the orders of the Secretary of War, the sentences will be duly executed under the direction of the general commanding the Department of the Columbia, at Fort Klamath, Oregon, Friday, October 3, 1873.

WM. W. BELKNAP,
Secretary of War.

BIBLIOGRAPHY

Bellows Falls Times, Bellows Falls, Vermont; various issues, June-October, 1873.

The *Morning Call,* San Francisco, California; various issues, June-October, 1873.

The *Chronicle,* San Francisco, California, various issues, June-October, 1873.

Eureka Times, Eureka, California; various issues, June-October, 1873.

Evening Bulletin, San Francisco, California; various issues, June-October, 1873.

War With The Modoc Indians, 1872-1873; 43rd Congress, 1st Session; House of Representatives Executive Document Number 122; 1874.

Map and Chart Illustrations by Francis S. Landrum

All photographs except numbers 40 and 125 are from the files of the Shaw Historical Library, Klamath Falls, OR.

Printed by
Maverick Publications
Bend, Oregon